Stilettos No More

*To Karyn,
who helped make this
book possible!

Diana
Estill*

Also by Diana Estill

Deedee Divine's Totally Skewed Guide to Life

Driving on the Wrong Side of the Road

Stilettos No More

Diana Estill

Stilettos No More

For information about special discounts for bulk purchases, contact:

Totally Skewed Productions
120 E. FM 544, Suite 72, PMB 135
Murphy, TX 75094

ISBN-13: 978-0-9799708-5-6

ISBN-10: 0-9799708-5-7

Library of Congress Control Number: 2010917519

1 2 3 4 5 6 7 8 9 10

First Print Edition

www.TotallySkewed.com

For every woman who's ever suffered a
wardrobe challenge

Contents

Minor Details, Major Blunders

Managing the Optics

Hollywood Hazards

Holiday Survival Skills

Bonus Story

INTRODUCTION

Sooner or later, this milestone moment occurs for all of us. We try on a pair of pumps with four-inch heels and realize the only way we can wear them is to remain seated. Or we slide into that little black dress that's been in the back of the closet and find that to make it fit we must first bind our hips with Lycra. That's when we break down and, under a cloak of secrecy, head to the mall to purchase a "body slimmer"—a garment with a name that suggests false benefits. But let's face it; no one would buy this contraption if it was more accurately labeled "fat concealer."

This book is about the period of life when new and often unwelcome awareness pushes past years of blissful denial, the times when a gal arrives face to face with the magnifying side of her hand mirror only to discover 50 is *not* the new 40. She's likely never again going to look 40. At least not without the help of Botox, a plastic surgeon, or Photoshop.

But that's OK. She's also never again going to have to ask anyone if her butt looks too big (nobody ever specifies for what) in any outfit . . . because she already knows the answer. AND she owns a body slimmer.

If you're a 30-something-year-old who snickers at these ideas, then all I have to say to you is, keep reading. You can't change the inevitable, but you might want to be better prepared for what awaits you.

For everyone else, please know that I'm not laughing at *you*. I'm laughing at *her*, the girl in the preceding paragraph. She still thinks she'll escape, unscathed, with a defined waistline. Twenty-five years ago, I thought so too. Today, however, I own *two* body slimmers and not a single pair of stilettos.

PAINFUL TRUTHS

Breakfast at I-STOP

I can't tell you exactly when it happened. Probably it occurred sometime between that first chin hair and my transition to stretch-fit jeans. But somewhere along the way I started to look my actual age, as opposed to behaving like it. This became painfully evident one Sunday morning while I was having breakfast at a place I now call "I-STOP," as in "I stopped eating there."

"What'll you have," a waitress asked me.

"I'd like the carb carcinogen combo," I replied.

"And you, sir?" she said turning to my husband. With her pen she scrawled something on a notepad the size of an index card.

"I'll have the monster meal, with the eggs scrambled," he replied.

"Oh, doesn't mine come with eggs, too?" I inquired. If so, I needed to let her know that I didn't want a sunny runny embryo on my plate.

The server looked at me for a split second before she answered. "No. There aren't any eggs on the Senior Plate."

I froze momentarily and tried to rewind the audio. Did she just say "*senior?*" One glance at my spouse confirmed that I had heard correctly. He now appeared to be searching for a safe escape route.

I checked my attire, but that helped explain nothing.

Am I not wearing flare-leg jeans? Is this not a hip-looking shirt? Aren't my earrings dangly and sterling? What is wrong with this woman? Do I look like a blue-haired, penny-saving, don't-bring-me-none-of-that-boysenberry-syrup senior customer? And how come she didn't ask hubby if HE'D ordered the senior portion?

I felt my face grow flush. Or maybe it was just another hot flash.

Did I forget to apply my concealer this morning? Can she see my roots from where she's standing? How would that be possible, given the lighting in here is one notch up from an appliance bulb?

"I didn't order a senior meal," I politely corrected.

"Oh, I'm sorry. Then, yes. How do you want your eggs?"

Briefly I considered saying, "On your face will be just fine."

We didn't talk about it while I sawed at my cold French toast and hubby chased congealing hash browns across his plate with a fork. It felt as though something tragic had just happened, something so fresh and raw that to speak of it would have been almost life-threatening, especially had the first comment come from my baby-faced spouse's lips.

We paid no further mind to the rude, undiplomatic, and obviously sight-challenged waitress. Though I might have enjoyed it, it simply wouldn't have been right to have made fun of someone who warranted her own telethon.

The drive home from the restaurant was exceptionally quiet. Minor chitchat dominated what little conversation took place. But when I entered the comforts of our suddenly geriatric-looking home, I turned to my spouse and said, "Did you hear that waitress call me a *senior*? Am I really a senior now?"

My man bowed his head and stared at the floor tile before he replied, "Yes."

"I am?" I cried.

"I'm afraid so."

"Gosh. I didn't think we looked like seniors," I said, slowly succumbing to reality. "I mean, she didn't even mention the senior meal to *you*."

"I know! And I was hoping she would too," said my breakfast companion, "because I wanted the discount!" He thought for a second and then with a grin added, "You know, I got carded this week when I bought a bottle of wine." He gave a conceited horselaugh.

If I'd had a walker, I'd have clobbered him with it.

I paced the room for a bit. And then I remembered something about space travel, which, on the surface, might not seem related to feeling old. However, given the way my mind works, this was relevant. "Well, Einstein had a theory about time and travel," I said. "He believed that if people could just go fast enough, faster than the speed of light, they could stop or even reverse the aging process."

Hubby furiously churned his feet and pumped his arms.

"What are you doing?" I asked.

"I'm trying to go that fast!" he said. Then he clutched his chest and gasped. "But I think I better go lie down." He heaved a deep breath and sighed. "I wore myself out."

I nodded. "Yeah, it's not safe for *seniors* to overdo it."

Failure to Act Your Age May Cause Injury

One advantage of having grandchildren is that they allow us to see the world anew through the eyes of a child. OK, maybe a youngster with blurred vision and poor memory—but a kid nonetheless. Don't bother trying to explain this to a childless woman under 30. Especially if she happens to be an emergency room physician quizzing you about an injury.

"It happened when I was going down a slide," I said.

"A slide?" the doctor parroted. She wrinkled her brow and squinted. I could almost hear her questioning my intelligence. She glanced at the chart in her hand. "What kind of slide?"

"A big one. A super slide. The kind they have at the state fair." I checked her expression. It hadn't changed. "Haven't you ever been on one?"

The stoic expert shook her head, indicating she hadn't. Of course not. She'd probably learned not to do this in Stupid Injuries 101.

"Well, it's really quite fun—when you don't get hurt," I mused. "It's very tall, and it has these humps in it . . ." I made a wavy motion with my hands. ". . . and you go terribly fast when you slide down it because you're sitting on a blanket that increases your velocity, or inertia, or whatever the scientific term is for that. Anyway, I was traveling about 60 miles per hour when I felt something crack."

The doctor looked at me as though she might next order a complete psychiatric workup. "Why would you do that?" she asked.

I shrugged. "My 10-year-old granddaughter."

The physician stared blankly, quite possibly waiting for me to say something close to normal.

"She wanted me to ride it with her, so I did."

Apparently unsatisfied with my explanation, the woman in the white coat said nothing.

"It was a *slide* for goodness sake! How do you get hurt on a slide?"

"You're not 10," said Doctor Smarty-Pants. "Let's get some X-rays."

You could argue that when my granddaughter Hannah asked me to accompany her, I should have known better than to say "yes." But you haven't seen those big, sad puppy eyes of hers. I'm serious. A local artist had just painted Hannah's face to look like a cartoon dog's mug.

I glanced at her and then looked up at the giant, multi-lane, metal behemoth before us. In an earlier day, this had been one of my favorite fairground activities. That was before Hannah's dad, Ron, had been born. Now I was nearly 40

15

years older and more than 50 pounds heavier, and in that stage of life where mass plus speed equals disaster.

We began our ride by ascending what from the pavement looked like a few flights of stairs but in fact necessitated enough stamina to hike the Himalayas. At first, there were steps. Then there were none. In between the stair flights were long metal ramps with 40-degree inclines. The higher I rose, the more distance (and steps) I could see ahead of me.

"Oh, yeah, Deedee," I forgot to tell you about these," Hannah said, indicating one of the slanted ramp sections. "They're kind of hard to walk on."

Seeing as that I was wearing flip-flops and using the handrail like a pulley to hoist my way to the top, I had to agree. However, I was gasping too hard to speak.

At the upper platform, two middle-aged men greeted me with a grin. One of them tried to hand me a wool blanket. "No thanks," I said between gulps for air. "Believe me, I'm not cold."

"It's to *slide* on," said the other guy. "You *have* to use it."

I bent over at the waist and held up one hand. "Could I just have a minute to catch my breath?" I begged. "I want to have enough left to scream."

The men nodded. Then they gave each other a knowing look.

I'd no more than sat down when both the blanket and my body unexpectedly shot off like I'd been fired from a canon.

In the lane next to me, and already yards ahead, Hannah zipped along on her back, her arms crossed like a mummy's.

I felt completely off balance. But I didn't dare try to imitate my granddaughter for fear I'd wind up with a fractured skull. My opposite end, I reasoned, was better padded for protection.

It then became obvious why those two slide operators were smiling. They must have given me a piece of greased fabric. Images from the movie *Christmas Vacation* flashed before my eyes. I recalled Randy Quaid's character, Eddy, rocketing through a retail strip center on an oily, spray-coated sled, sparks flying.

Trying my best to cant forward, I found I couldn't. Gravity and momentum held me captive in a partially-reclined position.

Somewhere about the third slide ripple, the impossible happened. I became airborne.

When my fanny next touched tin, pain shot up my tailbone. Right about then, Ron, who had intelligently remained where I should have stayed, took my picture. Later, he showed me the photo of my hilarious expression.

"Were you scared?" he taunted.

"Yeah. I was afraid I might never walk again."

As it turned out, my fractured tailbone healed in about six weeks. But the humiliation lasted *much* longer.

The pain was annoying, but the meds were pretty good. Mostly it hurt when I sat (roughly 90 percent of the time) and when I had to admit that my bones are brittle. And that I'm no longer 10.

Lest you think I'm the only family member who can't refrain from childish acts that lead to adult injury, let me dispel that belief. A year after I broke my butt (as my kids were fond of saying), my husband performed an even sillier stunt.

This episode began with a phone call from my dad, who has an annoying habit of calling me on weekend mornings before 9:00 a.m. Now, I love my Dad, but I really don't care to hear from anyone before I've had my morning caffeine, read the newspaper, and recovered from my trek from the bedroom to the kitchen.

To complicate matters, I come from a family with a seemingly endless capacity for drama. When Dad calls, often the reason is to share some piece of news I've previously been fortunate enough to avoid. So what I'm trying to say here, in the nicest way possible, is that Dad's phone calls are not always cheerfully received.

On this morning, the time was 7:45 a.m. when Dad telephoned. My husband Jim and I had just sat down to eat breakfast when the call arrived. I clicked on the speaker phone. This permitted Jim to join in the mind-numbing discussion about one of my kin borrowing money from another family member. To my father, this kind of information ranks right up there with CNN breaking news.

As Dad prattled on, I noticed Jim pantomiming next to me. He looked like he was fashioning something in his hands.

I glimpsed his antics.

Great, I'm getting a double dose of nonsense this morning.

". . . and you know he didn't have the money to lend," Dad continued.

"Probably not," I muttered between bites of toast.

Jim pretended to put a loop of something around his neck.

Changing the subject, Dad blurted, "Say, I bought a book for you to read. It's written by a dead senator."

"Wow, I didn't even know dead people could write," I replied.

Jim stepped onto the chair next to me and pretended to be holding a noose.

Dad ignored my previous remark and chattered on about the senator. "He has the best views and ideas of anyone I've ever read," he said. "So I bought an extra copy of the book for you, one for your son, and five for the library."

I tried to ignore the fact that Dad has never bought a copy of *my* book for anyone. Perhaps this is because, unlike many elected officials, my theories are intentionally humorous.

"Uh-huh. Thanks. That's nice." I managed to lie.

Standing in his chair, Jim waited to make eye contact with me. Then he jumped off the seat, causing both his bare feet to smack hard against the floor tiles.

He laughed and then grimaced.

I stifled a guffaw. But Dad sensed my mood and suddenly said he had to go.

Jim rubbed at his neck for the rest of that day.

Over the following weeks, my wannabe mime developed excruciating shoulder and arm pains. And a few months later, he underwent surgery to have two spinal discs fused.

Some laughs come at a great cost.

Now, I realize that expressing sideways anger is destructive and childish. Nonetheless, I've yet to read that dead senator's book.

Code Red Apple

One Friday morning, I read the newspaper and culled through the sale ads until two words caught my attention: "Red Apple." My pulse quickened. I exhaled slowly, sighing.

I could not afford to spend another dime on anything that wasn't an essential need. Not in this recession. But this was the summer clearance sale of the season, a signal for women to drop everything and meet at Macy's, the equivalent of deer season opening day for hunters—only with a much higher sense of purpose.

Like any addict, I did the responsible thing. I called a friend, someone who would encourage me to remain strong while battling my inner demons.

My neighbor and I had bemoaned our vows to curtail discretionary spending and save more money. So I knew exactly who to telephone.

"Macy's is having a Red Apple Sale," I said as soon as Colleen answered. She could, no doubt, hear the dread in my voice. "And shoes are SIXTY-FIVE PERCENT OFF!" I cried.

"When?" she asked.

"NOW! Right now! And they have the *cutest* sandals in their ad. I'm feeling like I might go," I confessed.

"I wear a size eight. Call me if you see anything good!" she begged.

So now I *had* to go because I'd assumed a responsibility to report findings.

Inside Macy's, I crouched between shoe racks sorted by size but not style. There truly was something here for everyone, from hoochie mamas to soccer moms. Four-inch stilettos? Yep, they had some. Rainbow print platforms? Uh-huh. Smart career pumps? Yes! Granny grips? Those too. And, of course, sandals!

I tunneled my way through rows of six-foot tall racks, peering deeply into the recesses of the bottom rungs. Patiently I waited for other hunters to snare their picks before I skillfully plucked off styles they'd surely missed.

Yes! I found a 7 in this one! Ee-ah-ha-ha-ha-ha!

Within a few minutes I'd snagged my quota. Well, OK, maybe more than my quota, seeing as how my self-imposed limit had been *none*.

Next, I wandered over to the size 8 section. Colleen was in luck! I found a flashy turquoise (her favorite color) patent leather sandal in her size. With my free hand I used my cell phone to call her.

"You've got to come see this shoe! It's an extra 10 percent off the sale price, so that's like 75 percent off, until one o'clock. I'm not good with math, but I think it's marked down to 12 dollars!"

"I'll be right there," she said.

By the time Colleen arrived, the crowd had increased in both number and collective euphoria. Four shoe clerks were about 10 short of being enough to service what appeared to be the most congenial shoppers in the world. Ladies who'd never before met one another now compared shoe finds and offered guidance.

"Where'd you find *that* style?" one woman asked.

"Right over there!" replied another.

"I saw that one and *thought* about it. It looks so cute on *you*, now *I'm* going to go back and get it," a stranger said to Colleen. The lady returned with a size 10 in the same style that Colleen had been modeling.

A female past a certain age sat in a chair, fondling two unmatched pumps. Each shoe sported a three-inch heel that looked like it could wreck hopes for an active retirement. The rest of us eyed her suspiciously. Surely no one her age would wear those bunion builders!

"Oh, nooooo. I still love my stilettos," the woman cooed. "I wear 'em to church and then take 'em off. But I *do* still wear 'em," she explained. "I don't care if they hurt. They look good on my feet. And I wait all year for Calvin *Kleins* to be 20 dollars! So I will sit right here as long as it takes for that lady to find the mates to these."

"Do these two leopard print ones look too much alike?" Stiletto Lady's pal said to anyone who'd volunteer an opinion.

"No," said three customers standing nearby.

"Yes," remarked Senior Stilts.

These two must have been related. I'm pretty certain only a relative would try to talk you out of a good shoe that's been marked down 75 percent, which is exactly why I hadn't called any of my kin.

I've now developed what I refer to as my financial security alert system. And the highest risk warning is "Red Apple."

Pain in the Pumps

The lady in the Calvin Klein pumps confounds me. I wonder how anyone over the age of 50—including Oprah—can still wear stilettos. Women like them must have taken better care of their feet than I. Or else they have a much higher threshold for pain, which is to say they don't cry every time a doctor orders a blood test.

In less than a decade, I've advanced from strutting in stilettos to longing for crepe-soled loafers. My feet have been permanently altered by years of fashion following. I was dumb enough to fall for the hype that suggested "hot" women wear high heels. Believe me, there's no truth to this. I'm overheated right now, and I'm barefoot.

Men supposedly get a lift from looking at gals who're wearing three-inch pumps. But I've concluded the only guys who notice women's shoes are the ones who want to borrow them.

All this agony my toes have suffered never brought me an ounce of male attention—other than from a few podiatrists.

In my youth, I wore spike heels to make my legs look shapely. Those shoes might have worked great for my calves, but they turned my feet into heifer hooves.

I'm telling you all this to explain why I purchased a promising medical aid that I'll refer to here as "Torture Toes."

Supposedly, after wearing these devices several hours each day, my feet will return to their natural shape, to the way they looked before I forced them into countless days of confinement in pointy-toe, elevated footwear that made me prance like a proud pony and left me hobbling like a lame horse.

When my toe spreaders arrived, I excitedly put them on. I'd ordered a size "S", which I thought stood for "Small" but must have indicated "Sasquatch."

Twenty seconds after I'd smashed my feet into these miracle cures, I lost all sensation below my ankles. Minutes later, when the feeling returned, I felt like someone was ripping me apart, one little piggy at a time! If militaries ever discover this product it will be used in place of waterboarding.

Soon after I'd firmly secured my toe spreaders, a searing pain radiated up both legs. I chewed my fingernails. Then I bit my cuticles. Now I understood why trapped animals sometimes free themselves by gnawing off an appendage.

"Ou-ou-ouch!" I yelled. "I can't take this another second!"

My husband, who was seated comfortably next to me in his reading chair, looked up from a novel. Evidencing his keen observation skills, he asked, "What's wrong?"

"These things are KILLING me!" I bounced my heels on the ottoman in front of me, keeping time with the throbbing pulse I could now feel in both knees.

Ever the caring spouse, hubby replied, "Don't worry. I'll take them off you if you pass out."

"Oh, you are too kind," I snapped. "Why don't *you* try wearing them?"

"I don't need to wear them," he said. "I've never worn high heels."

"Well, I bet you couldn't make it twenty minutes in these things."

"Sure I could. Give 'em here."

I released my tootsies from their imprisonment and handed over the challenge.

Wise Guy claimed the Torture Toes were too big for him too. But eventually he managed, with my help, to cram them onto his bunion-free feet.

Moments later, I noticed him eyeing the bedroom clock. "How long has it been?" he asked.

"Not twenty minutes," I replied. I shot him a victory smile. "Hurts, doesn't it?"

"It tingles a bit."

To prove his point, hubby wore the Torture Toes exactly 26 minutes—just long enough to beat my time. Then he took them off and declared, "The numbness finally stopped."

I located the Torture Toes carrying pouch and read the attached instructions. "If numbness or burning occurs, discontinue use."

It's a shame stilettos don't carry the same warning.

Athletic Shoes Shouldn't Cost More than Tires

"Hey, neat shoes," I said to my daughter-in-law Julie.

"Yeah, I just got 'em," she replied, jutting out one foot to exam it. "They're Avia's."

I tried to think which of her friends was named Avia.

Julie noted my expression. "You know . . . the *brand*?"

"No, I don't know athletic shoe brands. I buy a pair once every four or five years," I confessed. I kicked out one leg, offering a wrecked Reebok shoe for inspection. "I think I got these back in 2004, when I went to Disney World with you guys."

"Mom!" my son the competitive runner chimed in. "Don't you know you're supposed to replace your running shoes every *six months*?"

"Why?" I asked.

"Because you break them down, wear 'em out."

"Only if you do something strenuous in them, like *run*," I clarified.

"No," he insisted, "even if you're just *walking* in them."

"But I'm mostly walking indoors, on *carpet*," I explained. To damage soles, I figured I'd need to do something athletic—like clean out the garage.

According to what I've since verified from an Internet search, my shoes could have aged before I ever bought them. It's possible I've had a sort of "dead shoe walking," if you will. One website suggested that the glue already could have been drying out and the air pockets dissipating before my footwear ever left the store shelf.

I had to admit the only thing I wanted to find deflated about my sneakers was the price.

The article I read suggested asking the sales clerk how long the sports shoes had been in the store. But given the current environment, I suspect it would be difficult to find a salesman who's been on the job longer than the merchandise has been on sale.

One report I checked said that running (or in my case, shuffling) shoes should be replaced every 500 miles. I did the math. I walk about 15 miles per week, when I get motivated. That happens only when the outdoor temperatures climb above 50 degrees, or after I've eaten a platter of pasta, or when I discover I can no longer fit into any of my chairs. Running is confined to times when I'm being pursued by dangerous dogs.

By my calculations, I should be able to go nine months before wearing out a pair of sneakers.

At a cost of roughly $60 a pair, if I follow the 500-mile replacement rule, by the time I've walked 50,000 miles I will have spent $6,000 on athletic shoes.

So my question is simply this; if a set of auto tires that cost $600 will carry me 50,000 miles powered by a gasoline engine, then why the heck should I pay 10 times that much for tread to help me *walk* the same distance?

Even after factoring in fuel cost, it's cheaper to drive than use my own two legs. And I'll always prefer a vehicle's advantages to my physical limits. Especially when there's a loose Rottweiler headed my way.

Excuse #964: With shoe prices at current levels I simply can't afford to exercise.

Better Than a Gym Membership

Answers to weight loss can be so simple that we overlook them when they're right at our feet. Literally. In fact, they could be as close as the nearest superstore.

In search of several items, I arrived at a major discounter's door with a list: fitness video, elastic workout bands, petroleum jelly, prepackaged salad, and (don't judge me) a chocolate bar.

First, I sought out the exercise video. Pushing my buggy through the maze of DVD offerings, I found no fitness category.

But wait a minute. It's January. Doesn't every retailer have a good supply of workout videos this time of year? Perhaps I've overlooked this instructional section. Or maybe they've included the fitness videos in the more appropriate area, under "Fantasy."

A circle back through the entertainment aisles proved both my guesses wrong.

Up ahead, a young man wearing a red shirt casually relocated products from one shelf to another. "Excuse me," I called to him. He raised his head and looked as me quizzically. "Can you tell me where the workout videos are?" I asked. I tugged on my shirttail because I didn't want the guy to see the extent to which this question was overdue. But, to my dismay, there's only so much a yard of fabric can cover.

The employee who looked to be in his mid-20s extended one arm and pointed. "They're in the sporting goods section, at the far back," he said.

Then he added, "And there's more over in seasonal, opposite corner of the store."

Great. To find a fitness aid, I would have to *walk* a half mile.

Wouldn't it have been more practical to have placed these DVDs at the front of the store with the other videos, all in one spot, like, say, maybe close to the cookbooks?

I stumbled across the elastic workout bands I'd wanted while I was in "sporting goods." The fitness video I'd sought had been shelved two blocks away, in "seasonal." Now I was ready to locate the chocolate. And as luck would have it, I was already near the Valentine's Day candy. I congratulated myself on my shopping efficiency despite the store's disorganized layout.

But the chocolate I desired wasn't among the Valentine's Day items. And it wasn't in the bulk candy aisle, near the front of the store, either. In fact, I located the coveted bar in the grocery department, about 50 steps away from the prepackaged salad fixings. What luck! No circle backs required for the lettuce.

Now that I'd traipsed this gargantuan store from end to end a few times, I embarked upon the pharmaceutical area. If I couldn't find the petroleum jelly I needed for my hands, maybe I could at least pick up some pain reliever for my now aching back.

Neither the pharmaceutical nor the lotion and cleanser shelves contained the protective lubricant I needed. How hard can it be to find Vaseline? I wondered.

Behind an enclosed area, a lone woman filled prescriptions. She seemed oblivious to my sighs of frustration. Most likely, she'd become desensitized to customer confusion. Finally, I succumbed and asked her for directions.

"Can you tell me where to find the Vaseline?" I asked. "The plain, old, garden variety jars of petroleum jelly," I clarified.

"Check the baby products area," the pharmacist directed.

"Which way is that?"

Her head now bent over a pill jar, she casually offered, "Opposite corner of the store."

I wanted to go the direction she'd indicated. But I was simply too tired to perform another buggy lap. I'd get the Vaseline next time, when I remembered to wear my athletic shoes.

Waiting in the checkout line, fatigued from my all procurement efforts, I considered foregoing the workout video too. I mean, why should I pay for something that I can get every day in this store for free?

Mind over Bladder

It's no secret why women in later life gain weight. Aside from the natural declines in hormones and metabolism, that is. It's simple math. We can no longer walk as far as we used to go without having to stop and pee.

First we're children with walnut-size bladders, then we're pregnant women with pressing urges, and then when we think we've finally outgrown the need to schedule our days around potty breaks, midlife delivers the final kidney punch. Yes, I'm talking about the medical condition commonly known as the "gotta goes."

To build stronger bones, I've been trying to walk three miles a day. A couple of neighborhood lady friends in their 50s and 60s join me on my daily trek. Invariably, we stroll to about the two-mile mark before somebody makes like a Little Piggy and has to go "wee, wee, wee, all the way home."

This morning, it was my turn. "Uh-oh," I said, clutching my lower abdomen.

Colleen cut her eyes at me. "It's your turn today. It was mine, yesterday," she said.

I bit at my lower lip and nodded.

"Why don't you keep going straight when I make the turn," she said, indicating the shortest path back to my place.

"Already thinking that."

I picked up the pace. We power walked in silence. Then I began to pant.

"What are you doing?" Colleen asked.

"Panting," I replied. "It works during childbirth, doesn't it?"

"Yeah, it works to bring *on* the contractions."

I knew something about that hadn't felt right. I inhaled deeply through my nose and exhaled slowly from my mouth. "There. That's the breath used for pain management. And what I'm feeling right now qualifies."

"There's a Port-O-Potty up ahead," said my friend. "Why don't you run in there?"

"No way! I'd rather wet myself."

My walking buddy laughed. "Are you sure you're going to make it?"

"It's just mind over bladder," I quipped.

43

She waved goodbye as she made the turn on what would have been my normal trail.

I hastened my steps.

In through the nose, out through the mouth. In through the nose, out through the mouth. In through the nose, DO NOT COME OUT THROUGH THERE!

The park was almost in sight. I needed only to stride another four blocks to home. Drawing closer, I tried to distract myself.

See the verdant grasses. DON'T LOOK AT THE DEW on the blades. Drink in . . . no, don't DRINK IN ANYTHING . . . OK, just look at the calming pond. NO, NO! DON'T GLANCE AT THE FOUNTAIN!

My gait increased to a near jog. After I'd jaunted by the park, I needed only to race past 10 or so more houses to get home.

Yes! I had a visual lock on my target. Well, maybe not my *real* target. Just the door leading to the porcelain bull's eye.

OH, NO!!!

My neighbor's lawn sprinklers kicked on. An arc of spray mist fired my way. I forced a tighter Kegel squeeze and hoped not to wet my socks.

Look the other way, other way, OTHER WAY!

I glimpsed a wrought iron gate leading to a pool owner's back yard. Their Jacuzzi fountain squirted and bubbled like freshly uncorked champagne!

Bladders must have eyes because, as soon as I reached my front door, mine relaxed—before I was ready to let go.

I made a beeline for the guest bathroom. In my haste, I inadvertently switched on the fan instead of the light. But to find relief, I really didn't need to see (just something that rhymes with that).

In the dark, with the bathroom fan purring overhead, I contemplated my exercise regime. Perhaps I should get to know whoever lives in that house that's exactly two miles from mine. At the very least, I need to walk later in the mornings when everyone has turned off their lawn sprinklers.

DISAPPEARED INTO THIN HAIR

Comfort Should be King and Queen

When it comes to underwear, I have to ask: Is it OK to turn your briefs inside out and wear them a second time? Just kidding. Everyone knows the answer to that question, which of course is, "It depends." And I think it goes without saying that if your drawers *are* Depends, then the answer is definitely "no."

But what I really want to know is this: What makes boxer shorts *hip* and Mee-maw panties hideous?

It's suspicious to me that men are encouraged to wear comfortable underwear yet women are persuaded to sacrifice their bottoms for style. Come on. Full coverage is still full coverage, regardless of who's displaying it. We females already endure high heels, pantyhose, and chest binding constrictions that men, as a rule, don't suffer. Isn't that enough? Can we get an "amen" when it comes to selecting suitable skivvies?

I don't know how men's boxer shorts became currently popular. My grandfather wore boxers. The ones sold in stores today look no different from his. Nothing about these BVDs has changed in decades. Well, OK, nothing but the prices and boys' eagerness to show them off.

Meanwhile, men's regular briefs have been assigned detrimental names like tighty-whities to convince ladies that they ought to prefer the looser fitting varieties. And we've fallen for this nonsense. Worse yet, the same advertisers who suggest men's ugly undies are sexy have somehow managed to trick us into believing that thong panties are suitable for everyone from middle school girls to middle age moms.

Ladies, you have to admit that thongs are not underwear. They're teasers. The first women to wear them (other than maybe indigenous tribe members) were pole dancers. At least *they* were being paid for their discomforts.

Aside from the constant wedgie inherent in the design, I can find many other reasons to shun stripper panties. Feminine hygiene requires so much more than fanny floss. And when the lights are on and everyone is sober, how many women (other than the ones in men's magazines and lingerie catalogs) truly appear attractive in a thong?

Some gals suggest thongs are a natural remedy for unsightly panty lines. They're generally the same ones who're flying their little decorative triangles like flags every time they bend over. More than one guy has been known to give a full salute. And I'm not just talking about a former President.

I say it's time to reverse the trends. Bring back the climb-to-your-waistline, full-cut panties, or at least their mid-rise cousins, and return the guys to their bikini briefs. I want my Jockey male models back, the ones who wore those low-rise fashion cuts and didn't mind showing a little thigh. We never see underwear ads like *that* anymore.

About the same time that women succumbed to the myth that comfort is king only for males and the advanced aged, we managed to lose another equally important, and no doubt related, clothing battle.

As ladies' undies all but disappeared, so did our swimwear. Furthermore, while our bathing suits were steadily becoming more revealing (and expensive), men's swim styles did the reverse. Jacques Cousteau-inspired beachwear gave way to hugely more forgiving swim trunks. Today's baggy swim shorts can double for fish seining nets. In one leg opening it's possible to catch an entire school of perch and still have room for a turtle.

While all of these changes were taking place, a massive conspiracy was launched to educate the shopping variety of our species on what's considered stylish. We were told the Olympic dive team look is out. But my fellow fashionistas, it isn't the *look* that's out. It's the Speedo on the wrong man—like say, maybe, your father—that's undesirable.

I hate to be the one to draw your awareness to the discrimination that's been taking place in the intimate apparel and swimwear industries. But someone had to do this, and I imagine you'll agree. Women have been putting up with this thong enough.

Shapewear

For those of us who've lost our youthful figures, the fashion world has a solution called the body slimmer or thigh trimmer, or what's often referred to by our intimate partners as "sex repellent."

You've likely seen these repulsive-looking undergarments modeled in magazines by stick-thin gals with snake hips. This is a trick to make you think that if you wear one of these suffocating Lycra casings, you too will look equally skinny and unselfconscious.

But don't be fooled. When you squeeze into a body slimmer, every time anyone attempts to put an arm around your waist you will jump like an NBA star. In fact, you'll do most anything to prevent others from noticing your middle is under more pressure than canned biscuits.

God help those around you if you should blow a strap.

Bursting a support strap is highly unlikely, though, as these items appear to be made by NASA. Body shapers can withstand tremendous stress, which is the only condition under which these garments are intended for use. But you must be careful. If you lower a body shaper strap before first unhooking the crotch section, you run an extremely high risk of being hurled into the path of a jetliner. At a minimum, you could lose an eye.

Ads for shapewear profess these nylon gadgets will return your hourglass shape, support your bust, and eliminate unsightly bulges. One manufacturer even offers a "power panty," which causes me to wonder if it seals in odiferous gasses—but I think that's still in development.

What really happens when you suit up in shapewear is this: Your butt will rise just far enough to make your waistline totally disappear, and your boobs will be jammed so high that they'll be resting on your collar bone. Your knees will appear to have been replaced by giant grapefruit. And you'll become one dress size smaller, though sadly two shoe sizes larger. Hey, what else would you expect? All that excess skin has to go *somewhere*.

Now, don't get me wrong. I love my two body slimmers because they allow me to wear form-fitting dresses I outgrew during my last carb binge.

When I have one on, I feel 10 pounds lighter. And when I take one off, I'm always careful to unhook the crotch first and hang on tight because I need both my eyes.

The Patio Dress

When a gal is beyond the help of a body shaper, the next best solution is the "patio dress." As much as I'd like to tout the benefits of these sack shifts, I honestly don't know anyone who wears them. Come to think of it, I've never seen one except in sales brochures. Surely someone buys them. Possibly shoplifters.

What gets me most about patio dresses is that, much like shapewear, these outfits are always modeled by women who are waifs. And these ladies are generally shown standing with one hand thrust inside a pocket, their spindly arms hidden beneath folds of grotesquely-printed fabrics, their short cropped hair swept to one side and tucked behind an ear, and their attire accessorized by flat sandals and button earrings that haven't been available anywhere since 1983.

On their faces these models exhibit a confident smile to mask any embarrassment. Next to these svelte beauties' images, the ads typically say something like "**Available in Sizes to 5X!**"

If there is a low point in any model's career, it must be accepting a patio dress gig. But if they feel silly while posing, unlike the rest of us, at least they're comfortable.

The Stimulant Package

My normally sunny, happy-go-lucky disposition has been completely destroyed by recent events. I feel hurt, angry, and lost. At times it's even difficult to get out of bed. My mattress is nearly four feet off the ground, so, technically, it's always hard for me to rise from it. But, as they say in the South, that's a whole "nuther" issue.

What I'm talking about here is serious. Way serious. It affects not only me but also every family member who comes into close contact with me, "Da Man O' Da House" included.

People grow mean when you take away the little pleasures in life, the ones they believe are essential to their well-being, like Dr Pepper.

Research suggests that diet sodas can make a body fat. So initially I switched from a daily consumption of four cans of Diet Dr Pepper to two of the real stuff, the kind with 150 calories and 40 grams of sugar per 12-ounce serving.

Ever since I made this transition, you could say that my heft has dramatically increased. You could say it and see what happens! I don't recommend doing that.

It's entirely possible that I'm gaining weight also from a less than strict diet. Regardless, 300 calories' worth of soda pop per day isn't exactly part of an effective weight management plan.

To compound my problems, I have friends who are what I can only in the politest of terms describe as health freaks.

Upon witnessing my refrigerator filled with, EGADS, high-potency soft drinks, meaning those laced with high fructose corn syrup, otherwise known as POISON to some, one pal had to avert her eyes. She'd just bestowed upon me a pound of Amish-made butter and some whole, hormone-free milk that had been cheerfully supplied by grain-fed cows with green lips. How could I possibly expect such wholesome foods to share shelf space with non-nutritious stimulants?

I'd heard it all before, how awful all these various food additives and unnatural ingredients can be for those who wish to maintain good health. For every study that says one of these culprits is bad, I can find another that touts its benefits. Frankly, if I eliminated from my consumption every food or beverage that's had a negative research finding, I'd die from starvation, dehydration, or reading too many health journals.

In any event, I decided to improve my health by giving up caffeine. For good. Essentially this means I've turned into a caged badger. A groggy one, but still.

The degree to which I've been addicted to caffeine and/or Dr Pepper is debatable. I'll admit this drink has been, since childhood, a necessary part of my day. However, hubby says it's more like this; if I could find a way to dispatch Dr Pepper through a mainline, I probably would.

"Your only hope is for someone to invent a Dr Pepper *patch*," he teases.

Possibly you're wondering how anyone could become this hooked on a soft drink. Let me just say that access to this stimulant has been essential enough that my spouse checks the fridge before bedtime every night, to insure that *he* will have a good tomorrow.

But that was then, and this is now.

Today is Day Five without caffeine.

Who is ringing my phone? Oh, it's him, Da Man O' Da House. Interrupt, interrupt, interrupt! He's probably calling to ask if I've yet drunk a Dr Pepper.

OK, I'm back. Right now, right this very second, I am aware that there are six unopened cans of Dr Pepper in my fridge, half a dozen opportunities for failure. And I can honestly state that I don't want one.

I want them *all!*

If I had a smidgen of willpower, I'd throw away that soda pop. If I had a vengeful heart, I'd give it to someone who's attractively thin. But I simply can't part with my liquid lust, my carbonated companions. Somehow, just knowing they're here soothes my sleepy soul.

I sit and scheme of ways to quench my thirst for the forbidden. How could I do this without my husband knowing I've cheated? Already I have fallen once and been caught.

"It was nothing," I told him. "Just a frivolous one-time swig." But he didn't believe me. The hurt and disappointment showed in his expression. He studied my thighs and said nothing.

Ah, but that sweet stolen taste still lingers on my parched slack lips.

How long am I going to keep these remnants from my wayward days? It's difficult to say. But I can tell you this much: Given the state of our economy right now, the most valuable part of my children's inheritance could be a six-pack of unopened antique soda cans.

What? You think there's something wrong with that? Well, tell it to someone who's had their caffeine!

Editorial note: As of Day 11, the author's refrigerator contains only five unopened Dr Pepper cans.

The Big "M"

As much as I hate to beat up on doctors, the truth is, once a woman nears the "Big M," she might as well not whine to a physician about anything during her annual checkup. No matter what her complaints might be, her doctor will likely dismiss them by telling her that she's either entering or in the midst of menopause.

This is kind of like seeing a fortune teller who says your luck is about to change. Of course it is! Nothing remains static. So it's pretty easy to be accurate when you're being this vague.

It can easily take a decade to pass through "the change." Therefore, being told that most every minor health symptom (no matter how wardrobe threatening) during this time is somehow related to menopause is more than an annoyance. It's a waste of your "health spending" dollars.

We interrupt this stream of consciousness writing to bring you the following important medical disclaimer:

I am in no way qualified to offer medical advice, so please consult your doctor if you're looking for anything other than absurd health opinions. A physician may give you even more bizarre instruction, but at least those recommendations will be offered by a professional who is properly insured.

So, like I was saying, save your medical co-pays and buy a personal hair trimmer. You're going to need it. But I'll get to that in a second.

Despite the frustrations of being told so, much of what occurs during midlife *is* attributable to hormone fluctuations. And that includes the appearance of unwanted hair and the loss of one's car keys.

First, it'll be only a lone dark spike emerging from your chin. But then, overnight, this hair will grow faster than the US deficit. You won't see it before bedtime and yet, by the next morning, this new arrival will be long enough to fashion into a pin curl.

The next thing you know, all sorts of fuzz and freak whiskers will erupt. And that's when a good hairstylist can be your best friend. Just make sure she's young enough to see well.

My hairdresser is a second pair of eyes scrutinizing my ever-changing appearance. She was the first person to call my attention to the billy goat beard I'd sprouted under my chin—a necklace of platinum-colored fringe framing my drooping jowls. This hair was so light and fine that, without my reading glasses, I couldn't see it.

In her diplomatic way, my stylist offered her best professional advice: "LET ME SHAVE THIS STUFF OFF!"

A few months later, when my hairdresser began fretting over something on my forehead, I feared the worst. Surely I wasn't going to have to start using BOTOX too!

While cutting my bangs, she paused and stared at me. With one hand she scooped my hair straight back and peered more closely.

I waited to hear the dire news, whatever it was.

With an index finger and thumb, she plucked at something.

I felt a tug on my forehead.

"Omigod," she exclaimed. "It's *attached!*"

Glancing up, I saw her pulling on a single strand of white hair that must have been four inches long.

When she finally stopped laughing, she said, "Do you want me to remove it?"

Briefly I considered leaving the sprout intact and saving it as a conversation piece. Imagine all the laughs such an oddity might generate. If I left it alone, once my bangs were in place, only my hairdresser and I would know the straggler wasn't part of my normal mane. But then I reconsidered and asked her to pluck the hormonally haywire hair. To whom would I have shown it, anyway? None of my friends see well enough to notice their own strays.

The Hair

At first there were only two in our marriage. But somewhere along the way a third party showed up. Unwittingly, I became one of a threesome during intimate trysts. There was me. There was him. And then there was the concubine hair.

The origins of this interloper have yet to be determined. We haven't even correctly identified its gender. "Mine or yours?" we'll ask each other. It's hard to tell.

Sometimes I find the loose lock in my mouth. Other times it's in his when we kiss, and then it sneaks into mine. Soon enough, one of us is frantically picking it from our teeth. Once the nuisance is gone, we attempt to rekindle the passion . . . until . . . it's there again!

I'll feel something tickling under my nose and grab to find it. But before I can catch up to it The Hair is gone. Vanished as mysteriously as it arrived.

My spouse will then sputter, blowing something from his lips. The Hair is back! "Where *is* that thing coming from?" he'll say. And then we both begin speculating until we are forced to admit the mood has "evaporated into thin hair."

He accuses me of having bangs that shed. (I haven't told him about the strand my hairdresser found attached to my forehead.) And I suggest he must be in need of a nose trim. This has happened so many times that now, at the first sign of a prickle, we both look at each other and in unison exclaim, "The Hair."

I don't know how much official research has been done on this subject. But I'm relatively sure this is one reason sex becomes less frequent after age 50.

Fuzzy Navels and More

While The Hair is hiding, it's apparently multiplying. Its offspring may show up most anywhere, including your navel, toes, and, yes, even rooted from your third eye.

Do you know that Biblical passage that states God knows the number of hair strands on each person's head? Well, this must be because He has allocated a fixed quantity to the human race and is keeping track. That's why every time a guy gets a bald patch, a woman somewhere gains a mustache. It's all part of the Grand Design, nature's way of balancing human follicles.

One day, when the light was just right (and I was foolish enough to be looking for more flaws), I noticed a fine layer of fuzz that had developed on my back. This stuff looked like the coating on an okra pod. And I was dumb enough to ask for a second opinion. "Come here," I called to my husband. "What's this blonde stuff on my back? Is that *hair*?"

He drew closer to study the situation. "Naw," he said. Right when I heaved a sigh of relief, he added, "That's not hair. It's a rug!"

So my advice is this: Don't call attention to what your man hasn't already noticed. This only gives him ammunition when you start needling him about his receding hairline or those unattractive ear sprigs that are begging to be braided.

71

We all need some extra maintenance as we near life's center mark. But there's no reason to point out how much more women require than men. For multiple reasons, it's best to keep guys in the dark.

Speaking of maintenance, beyond a certain age, it takes much longer to grow leg stubble. But before you get too excited about dispensing with fewer weekly ankle-to-knee trims, understand that you may have simply gone from shaving your legs to waxing your back.

Sandal Scandal

As if the aforementioned were not enough to make me want to take out an emergency loan for laser hair removal, I caught a glimpse of the strangest tufts of all: toe hairs. This happened while I was wearing sandals *and* reading glasses. Please don't ask what else I had on. I can't remember.

My first awareness came after my daughter purchased a pedicure for my 55th birthday. I'd decided to do something a little different and get my toenails painted sparkly zebra striped. Having seldom ventured beyond hot pink polish, I considered this act fairly adventuresome. To preserve the memory, I snapped a photo of my animal print toenails and posted the image on a social networking site where people actually find these type pictures interesting. Then I clicked on the photograph to enlarge it. And there they were in vivid coffee-colored curls.

From where had these wisps of masculinity come? Good grief. I was turning into a man, feet first.

Now, these were not the tiny blonde fuzzies I'd come to disregard on my arms, back and, most recently, neck. No-o-o. These were the type sprouts that could cause my feet to be mistaken for my husband's, except he has gecko toes that would be an obvious giveaway.

Dismissing further concern, I returned the photo to normal size and reasoned these hairs were visible only with magnification.

But today, exactly 11 days before my 56th birthday, I put on my readers and hiked up my right foot to check for blisters. And now I see the truth. To *me*, those hairs were obvious only with magnification. Normal-sighted folks could probably view them from across the street.

I'm in New York City right now. And as best I can estimate, I've been walking 10 miles per day—often in wide circles. I've hiked the city from seaport to seaport, traversed the same block multiple times while looking for a subway entrance, and canvassed entire neighborhoods in search of a Dr Pepper. I've covered the expansive Museum of Modern History and meandered through the Irish Hunger Memorial and taken pictures of the World Trade Center reconstruction project, and I've ventured over to the TKTS discount ticket booth on the opposite side of town from my hotel. But I've also digressed.

Anyway, while I was sitting here at the desk in my modest hotel room, massaging my sore feet, I witnessed those irritating toe hairs again. Only, I'll be menopausal if they hadn't multiplied. Now they're forming ringlets!

No, no, no. This is not happening. I refuse to walk around looking like an estrogen-deficient freak. I may not be in charge of my hormones, but I surely am in control of my shaver. I have a triple-blade disposable razor with me, and I darn sure know how to use it.

Without further regard, I grabbed my plastic shaving tool and took a few swipes at both big toes. That's when I realized the condition had spread to the adjacent tootsies on each foot. Another quick pass removed the sinister sprigs from those digits too.

After I'd moved on to less essential pursuits, I felt my toes stinging. That's when I surveyed my feet and found I'd been overzealous while removing those unwanted hairs. A river of scarlet now seeped from cuts on both feet. I'd not only nicked myself, I'd triple-sliced four toes. If I didn't stop the bleed, I might have to pay for carpet replacement.

I'd like to say that right then I felt stupid. But what I experienced was more akin to disgust. How can a company make such a dangerous implement and not consider the myriad of ways a gal might try to use it? Had the manufacturer no sense of product liability? Where was the warning label?

Not intended for use by women over 50, nearsighted individuals, or people who suffer from Werewolf Syndrome.

As I sat there applying pressure to the tops of both feet, I realized I was on to something. The inventor of the nose hair trimmer probably started in just this same manner! He or she must have first tried to trim stray nose hairs with an unsuitable object, like maybe electric scissors, and then a better way must have revealed itself during either an Edison moment or an emergency room visit.

Surely it's only a matter of time until I will walk into a CVS store and find the "Pedi-trim" available for $9.99. If you should see it before I do, just remember whose idea that was.

A Final Warning about Hair

Before you become traumatized by all this discussion about unwanted hair, let me share one last tidbit no one ever tells you: The fur in your nether regions will gradually move north after age 50.

While you have been busy studying the back side of your scalp for signs of female pattern baldness, your *coochie* has been covertly thinning. What a shock it is to discover that all this time you've been observing the wrong end!

It's not your fault. Nobody tells you to be on the alert for missing pubes. So how could you have known? But I'm telling you now, my friend, one day your *nookie* will look naked. Until someone devises a pelvic hair implant, there's nothing you can do about this. Except be thankful you no longer need to contemplate getting a *Brazilian*, which is not to suggest that you've ever entertained that thought. Certainly not within the past decade, right?

How Not to Become a Stereotype

When midlife arrives, we don't have to follow the crowd to the cafeteria. A wide number of choices exist between the golden arches and Golden Corral. But if we're not careful, we'll find ourselves eating corn casserole at 4:30 in the afternoon. It doesn't have to be this way. We could wait until at least 6:00 p.m.

Many of our choices are the result of doing what's expected—like claiming to floss when we haven't. We may even catch ourselves falling into predictable patterns that'll make others think of us as geezers instead of the fun-loving, sight-challenged, ample-bodied folks we are. Well, maybe we're not all ample-bodied. Perhaps I got that confused with what I'm drinking.

Anyhow, like I was saying, the last thing anyone wants to become is a stereotype. So to help you know if you're in danger, I've devised this simple test:

If you're guilty of 5 or more of the following acts, it could be time to rethink your habits:

- You bought yourself a Snuggie.

- Ninety percent of your blouses have three-quarter sleeves.

- You own a bird-print cardigan and actually wear it. In July.

- You can't recall what year you last received a Victoria's Secret catalog.
  (Note: Check with your spouse.)

- Given a choice between having your feet thrust into a hot charcoal pit or crammed into a pair of pumps, you'd pick the coals.

- While shopping for full figure styles, you've at least once caught yourself accidentally drifting into the maternity section.

- You own more than 50 pairs of socks.

- No one has ever given you a thong, even as a joke gift.

- When walking through your bedroom and into your den, you pass a dozen or more pairs of reading glasses and yet can't find a set.

- You react like a vampire to a wooden cross any time you lift your hand mirror and find it turned to the magnification side.

- At a red light, when a cute guy pulls up next to your vehicle and stares at you, your first thought is: "I'm about to be carjacked."

- When dining out, you select restaurants on the basis of lighting candlepower, early bird specials, and chair cushion padding.

- At least once, you've hidden your guy's ED drugs. And he failed to notice.

- You're much less focused on apparel to enhance your figure than on manicures to accentuate your jewelry.

- You're pretty sure Justin Bieber is a type of carpet.

Texting

Another way to prevent appearing as a social "has been" (aside from having a Facebook account with more than two friends) is to simply send text messages. I know none of your buddies are texting. So just text your grandkids. They'll think you're cool, and then they'll tell this to the other 3,000 people with whom they never speak but frequently text.

I don't understand what all the hoopla is about sending text messages. Who started this form of communication, anyway? For lack of a better answer, I blame Ryan Seacrest.

What's so great about typing on a keyboard the size of a Fig Newton? By the time I'd punch out a message on my cell phone keypad, I could have handwritten a letter and driven it across town. Why do folks send text messages, anyway? Isn't it simpler to pick up the phone and speak into it? If Alexander Graham Bell could see us now, he'd wonder why he didn't just leave us stuck with the telegraph machine.

New technological trends keep producing products I neither want nor understand. Here's another example: instant messaging.

"Why would anyone want to receive an instant message?" I asked my husband.

He looked like I'd just asked him why anyone would want a flat screen TV. Then he explained, as though talking to a 10-year-old, "Sometimes, when I'm at work, and I'm on a conference call, I instant message someone else. This lets me talk on the phone to one group while I'm online with another employee." He gave me a sympathetic smile. "It's a shame *you* don't have instant messaging. Then I could talk to you while you're working too!"

"No," I snapped. "That's the point. When I'm writing, I don't want to be interrupted. Besides, most of my stories are already confusing enough."

See, I don't care to have my brain yanked every time someone else needs immediate gratification, boredom relief, or proof of my devotion. There's a reason why I have this annoying feature disabled (instant messaging, not my devotion). Anyone who sends an instant message should simultaneously receive a mild electrical shock—one that's not injurious but rather just jolting enough to deter such discourteous behavior.

Individuals who walk around with their ears continuously plugged by a headset ought to be zapped once in a while too. Good grief. If constant tunes were the ticket to happiness, the MUZAK generation never would have stepped off an elevator. And if listening to nonstop talking made you smart, every parent of a six-year-old would be a genius.

Call me a relic, but I don't care to send text and instant messages. And, you know, I'd just as soon not "get the message," either.

MINOR DETAILS, MAJOR BLUNDERS

Just the Fats, Ma'am

If you've read this far, I think it's safe to presume that you want to know something gossip-worthy about me. So I'll come right out and confess. Today, I am writing my first all-nude story.

I realize you have no way to verify if I'm telling the truth. And if you do, please put down the binoculars now and turn yourself in. But trust me. I'm sitting here, right this second, just the way God made me—stripped of any cloth, my thighs lapping like fresh bread dough over the edges of my secretarial chair, breasts competing with my hands for the keyboard. Be glad there's no video linked to this book. What I'm revealing here is not a pretty sight (neurotic, perhaps, but not erotic). If being an author doesn't work out for me, maybe I can become a model for comical greeting cards.

See, I'd planned to keep it a secret that I work this way (not always, just when I'm doing laundry). However, because I won't dare shave my head bald, space out on illegal drugs (I'm loopy enough without them.), or starve myself to a size 0, there's little left for me to do to attract media attention. But wait. There's more to tell.

My lack of attire isn't the only information I've failed to divulge. In my younger life, I was raised by a team of mules. Or maybe they were just mule-headed people. Sometimes you have to tweak specifics for the sake of a good story. Anyway, one day I realized that, similar to a thoroughbred, I could easily sprint a quarter-mile. So I set off to become a champion runner. Unfortunately, I didn't make it past my third grade track team tryouts.

Having given up on becoming a competitive athlete, I next decided to train for a job at the racetrack. If I couldn't run fast enough, I'd ride something that could, namely, a derby horse. But I developed a slight weight problem, otherwise known as pregnancy, which prevented this dream from coming to fruition. I did, however, meet Mickey Rooney and ride the horse Seabiscuit before moving on to other careers. All right, maybe I only *saw* Mickey Rooney on TV and *read* the book, *Seabiscuit.* It's hard to remember the EXACT order of events.

During my late twenties, I developed a debilitating speech pathology that caused me to utter phrases like "I do" to the wrong people. This crippling affliction forced me to look for ways to heal myself, as Norman Cousins, author of *Anatomy of an Illness,* did: with laughter. Eventually, this led me to writing newspaper humor columns and essays.

Against the odds of possible failure and near certain poverty wages, I published my first book,

Driving on the Wrong Side of the Road: Humorous Views on Love, Lust, & Lawn Care. To promote that book and my future ones, I must now do something outlandish or sensational or scandalous. That's why I've decided to share my story with you here.

Next week, I'll be writing from an undisclosed rehab facility for women with compulsive eating disorders. Well, maybe it's a day spa. If you must have the precise details, it's my bedroom—but I'm removing all the chocolates. I'll still be writing in the buff, as opposed to writing, buff. (It's all in the semantics.) Media phone interviews, as always, are welcome. Clothing is optional.

My Dirty Little Secret

Often others ask me how I find the subjects I choose to write about. So here's the answer: After hours of staring at a blank page, trotting back and forth to the pantry for snack replenishments, checking my chin for new growth, and Google searching my own name, I resort to a special trick to find a writing subject. I turn to my idea notebook and cobble together something I call the "catch-all" story. You've probably witnessed many of these without knowing it. In fact, you couldn't have arrived at this page without passing a few.

My idea book is filled with years of research performed by someone other than me, someone who actually works hard for your tax dollars by writing grant proposals to garner more tax dollars. This information prepares me to address pointless and stupid questions, because I'm a highly trained professional who knows how to do this.

I sit around and contemplate the real need for household items like charger plates (a plate to hold your plate?) and quesadilla makers and wonder where mosquitoes go to ride out the winter. Do they all have second homes in southern Florida?

Sometimes I study serious matters, such as the relationship between stock values and corporate consciousness. A correlation does exist. It's just an inverse one.

I can't help but wonder why self-cleaning windows were invented before anyone thought of disposable curtains. And I'm perplexed by the MIT student who designed an alarm clock that can wake a person and then roll itself under a bed, out of sight. How is that break-thru technology? I've had something equivalent for years. It's called a cat.

It seems obvious to me that chiggers could be used in place of biological warfare. Imagine all the money that could save! The other side would immediately surrender.

And while I'm on the topic of saving money, wouldn't it be cheaper for men and women to share the same shaving creams? Other than the color of the cans, and maybe that passion fruit scent, who can tell the difference? I mean, besides folks who study profit margins.

Birthday parties puzzle me too. When, exactly, did it become necessary to throw toddler birthday bashes on an entertainment par with Ringling Brothers Circus? And why do we give children toy replicas of the very items we warn them not to play with (cell phones, computers, DVD players, credit cards, and ATM kiosks)?

Retailers' catalogs have provoked many more amusing thoughts. From studying men's underwear ads (Yes, I do, but I only read the labels.), you'd think most male models have a bad case of Shingles. They're usually pictured posing with their undershirts hiked up and their fingers clawing at their abs. Soooo, enticing! Underwear that'll make a guy scratch himself just like Fido.

But the female models look equally ridiculous with their "come hither" stares. By the way, have you noticed that all the ones who advertise shapewear lack any hint of a figure? Why would a gal whose body could easily be mistaken for an adolescent boy's need a girdle? Come to think of it, faces are seldom shown in those ads. I bet those models really *are* boys!

I've often tried to calculate how much kitchen counter space a gal would need if she owned all the gadgets inside one of those bed and bath shops. There's stuff in there that I can't identify, much less find incentive to use.

And speaking of things I can't identify, whose idea was it to put the turkey's innards (cleverly disguised as "giblets") in the neck opening and the neck inside the body cavity? I never know where to look for what, but I keep straight by remembering that turkeys are the birds with their heads stuck up their behinds.

By now I've fully demonstrated the art of the catch-all story. As a side benefit, I've also reached my word-count quota for the day. See how well this works?

Taxi Turmoil

"I was worried when I heard about the terrorist plot at JFK," my mother said. However, I'd flown into the New York area through LaGuardia Airport instead of JFK International. Home now, I thought it best not to tell Mom that the greatest risk to my safety had been waiting for me at the taxi stand.

I'd arrived in Manhattan psyched to attend BookExpo America, the largest publishing trade event in the US. While there, I'd had the chance to rub elbows, bellies, boobs, and behinds with 30,000 sweaty strangers. Attendees were sandwiched inside a cavernous funhouse full of publishers, authors, book buyers, and librarians—or at least people who pretended to know one.

New York City's Jacob Javits Convention Center is a monstrous glass structure that appears to have been designed by a dizzy architect. The second level is wedged, willy-nilly, in sections (keenly disguised as food courts) between the sprawling first and third floors. Thus, when an individual is inside this facility she can't ever be certain where she is—other than in the belly of a cash cow.

To distract visitors from navigational challenges, the interior of this building is kept at a perfect temperature for baking yeast breads. Further aggravating these conditions is the quantity of ladies' restroom stalls, which falls somewhere between insufficient and scarce enough to ignite a panty war. In other words, the place is pretty much ideal if you happen to be, oh, I don't know, say, maybe a prairie dog.

Preoccupied with finding my way around this enormous structure, I hadn't even known about the JFK fiasco until a day after the related news reports. Primarily, I'd been focused on surviving the convention and the streets of New York.

During one of my many cab rides, my driver, Ahmed (the first of three taxi operators I encountered who all either shared the same name or, possibly, the same license), flew through a tunnel as if the paparazzi were following us. Because I'm not famous, I felt sure they weren't.

Do you know how many lanes exist within a typical, one-way, New York City street? Answer: As many as cabbies feel like making.

Time Square roadways are clotted with busses, cars, bicycle rickshaws, horse carriages, and foot traffic that sometimes includes a naked singing musician, often all competing for the same lane.

Apparently, the NY School of Taxi Driving & Tourist Intimidation teaches a terrifying method for saving time and maximizing trip turns. Taxis generally keep to the far left on one-way streets, where they travel at car chase speeds, ignoring nuisances such as crosswalks, stoplights, and unarmed pedestrians. At the last possible moment, like maybe when he's an inch or so from taking out an unsuspecting vacationer, a taxi driver will whip his vehicle to the right, crossing three or more lanes, to make an abrupt though necessary directional change.

New York cabbies never use their turn indicators for fear of tipping off opposing motorists.

With a fiendish smirk, my driver explained, "It's like a game. "Whoever gets there first, goes." He shrugged. "You just honk and keep moving."

I nodded, indicating I understood. "Yes," I said, "we have those games in Texas too. One driver will cut off another driver, and then whoever pulls his gun first, shoots."

Busted in Boston

The shortest path to hypertension and poverty can be found by following a Google map—in a taxi.

I arrived in Boston, armed with a list of radio and TV interviews to conduct. At my hotel, the receptionist said, "I'm afraid we don't have the king size bed you requested." For consolation she offered me the Drunkard Suite—a room so small that I needed only to open the door and fall forward to land in the double bed. If the hotel room wasn't an indicator of what was to follow, my first telephone interview had to have been an omen.

Referencing a story I'd written about Irish history, my publicist had sent the radio host a news release that mentioned "Celtic pride." The interviewer had mistakenly thought I was a Boston Celtics fan. Owing to my lack of sports expertise, I'd been surprised to learn Boston had a team by that name.

After this major blunder, I rushed off to do a live interview at a nearby "oldies" station. My taxi driver, a nice young man from faraway lands, asked, "You know this place?" which I interpreted to mean, "Will you notice if I just drive you in concentric loops around the city while my meter runs like Seattle Sleuth?"

"No. I've never been there. But I have a Google map," I warned. "It should be *easy* to find."

We left the hotel during a major downpour. At first, the directions I'd been given made perfect sense. And then they didn't.

I called the radio station, but no one answered. Only 40 minutes remained until I was due "on air."

We made a few questionable stops before I spied what I thought must be the right location. "Stop here," I instructed the driver, "and please wait."

But once inside, the security guard set me straight. "No-o-o, this is a different radio station than the one you're looking for," he said. "We traded buildings with them a while back."

I did my best to relay the guard's instructions to the Meter Man. His black box with blinking lights now indicated a cab fee that could have covered air fare to Canada.

"What. Is. The. Street. Address?" he asked in his staccato voice.

"Leo Birmingham Parkway," I stressed for the kazillionth time. "We need to find Leeeeee-oooooooooo. Birrrrrrrrrr-miiiing-hammmm. Parrrk-waaaaaaaay."

"OK, I find it," he replied. "Don't worry."

Surely he had a Boston street map or someone in his home office who could help him find this road. I sunk into the back seat, confident he had a plan.

The cabbie eased up to a red light, honked his horn, and lowered his window. The driver next to us, a lone woman who looked to be in her sixties, strained to listen. "Do you know where is a Lay-oh

Bom-ang-hom?" my guide shouted, his accent thicker than day old grits.

The confused lady screwed up her face. "I'm sorry. What?" she asked.

"A LAY-OH BOM-ANG-HOM," shouted the taxi driver.

Immediately, the light turned green. The lady shook her head and drove away.

That was his plan? To stop traffic and ask frightened women for directions?

From there we traveled to an auto repair shop. Mr. Don't Worry stopped the car and went inside. When he returned, he said, "OK. I know where it is."

Several minutes later, we arrived in front of a towering communications center, and I jumped out, racing toward the studio, with two minutes to spare. However, to my dismay, I'd arrived in error at CBS television studios.

Eventually, we found the station—ten minutes past my air time.

Nearly falling into the radio offices, I was ushered to a chair and told to take a deep breath. A technician pointed to a microphone and said to the host, "Ready when you are." The DJ introduced me and, just like that, I went "live."

Outside, in the parking lot, Meter Man waited for my return. I hated to put my pocketbook on the critical list like that. But it was the compassionate thing to do, as I'm pretty sure that cabbie needed me to help him find his way back to downtown Boston.

Shades of Purple

Book tours can be grueling. For those who survive their publicity campaigns, bouts of fatigue accompanied by sudden acts of stupidity are not uncommon. These media events zap an author's energies, leaving him or her exhausted and spacey—if not dead. In the latter case, this only makes the writer's works more valuable. By my calculations, I'd have to die twice before my books will become worth the paper they were proofed on.

My last book tour caused me to become dangerously absentminded. As much as I hate to admit it, the following events are true. In accordance with HIPAA regulations, though, I'm prohibited from disclosing the victim's real name. Thus, I shall simply refer to her as "Miss Kitty."

Before anyone writes an accusatory letter to me, let me state right off that this incident caused my feline friend no permanent harm. She suffered only mild discomfort, albeit extreme disgust.

It all started when I asked my husband, deficient shopper that he is, to purchase some dry cat food for our pet. We needed to replenish supplies before leaving for an out-of-town book signing engagement. Desiring to get the correct brand, he asked the key question: "What color bag does it come in?"

"Maroon," I replied.

Now I realize this was a mistake. Anything other than a primary color, such as blue or red, was certain to throw him off track. Instead of maroon, I should have at least used a familiar term, like "wine."

When the aforementioned visually challenged shopper returned home, he carried inside a bag that appeared more purple than burgundy. I studied the sack. Like soda cans, maybe the packaging had been recently altered by the manufacturer. Hurriedly, I dumped a mound of morsels into Miss Kitty's bowl. She sniffed at my offering, gave me a look that suggested, "You've GOT to be kidding," and sashayed away with her tail fashioned into a question mark.

A few days later, I departed home, leaving Jackie, our outstanding pet sitter to care for my four-legged baby.

In Boston, I jumped when I saw Jackie's number identified on my cell phone. Probably Miss Kitty had become so distraught over my absence that she couldn't eat or stand. How could I have abandoned her this way? I'm her whole world, her entire reason for napping 37 times a day. I prayed she'd hang on until my return.

"Do you have some dry food," Jackie asked when I answered the phone. "I've looked all over and can't find any. All I see is a bag of dog food sitting here."

"Dog food? You found DOG food in my house? Are you sure it's *dog* food?"

"Oh, it's definitely dog food," she said.

"Do you mean to tell me I've been feeding my cat *dog* food?" I could feel the heat of embarrassment flooding my face. What kind of kitty keeper was I? "Please don't report me to Cat Protective Services," I begged.

Jackie laughed. "Oh, don't be so hard on yourself," she consoled. "You'd have noticed it sooner or later. It has a picture of Lassie on the front of the bag."

"It even has a picture on it?" I repeated, my voice spiraling higher. "Tell me you're kidding."

"Nope. It sure does, right here on the front."

I suppose things could have been worse. It's a good thing hamster food doesn't come in a seven-pound grape-colored bag.

Once home, I found two sacks of pet food—one purple, one burgundy—carefully situated on top my washing machine. A sticky note appended to each bag identified the package images. One said "CAT," and the other said "DOG."

It's good to have this kind of dedicated help.

Dog and Cat People

Along with forwarded email jokes, funny stories, and lucrative business proposals from Ubinspamistan, occasionally I receive anti-fan mail. It's hard to believe that a humorist could provoke hate mail. But believe me, it's even more difficult to comprehend how some of the authors of these messages have found, let alone summoned sufficient brain power to read, the columns they're griping about.

A sportsman once wrote to ask if I'd been serious about my dove hunting remarks. He'd read my critical comments in a column titled "The View

Askew." Perhaps the title's two-syllable word had surpassed his understanding.

To be clear, yes, I meant it when I said I was perplexed by anyone's desire to dress in heavy Special Ops-like clothing, abandon the comforts of air conditioning during late summer, and traipse across fields to find the symbol of peace . . . and shoot it. However, this behavior would be perfectly logical if you simply replaced the dove in the previous example with mosquitoes.

It's not only hunters who give me flack. I received three email responses from the same individual about a column I'd written five months earlier. Possibly it took her that long to assemble her thoughts. The reader expressed irritation over comments I'd made about my son's dog. She informed me that my grandpuppy was a breed for which she held a deep, abiding passion—and a public relations job to promote. Apparently, she was so on top of her duties that she didn't know how to set a Google alert.

"You've got to watch out for those dog people," a friend said when I relayed this story. A dog owner herself, she suggested my life could be endangered.

Ha! Humorists *laugh* at danger! Most of us are so affected that we laugh at everything! *We* are the spooky ones.

Nonetheless, allow me to set the record straight. I love animals—all kinds. In fact, my husband accuses me of caring for some of them way too much. I've been known to slam on my car brakes while driving on a six-lane roadway, in rush hour traffic, just to save a squirrel. (Or to respond to a shoe sale sign.)

Our house pet receives better treatment than some family members. I mean, I didn't allow my children to sleep in bed with me when they were preschoolers. Yet our ten-year-old cat wedges herself between me and my spouse every night.

When my feline companion gets underfoot, which is any time my husband or I become vertical,

I take heroic precautions to dodge her. The Mister, however, mistakenly thinks he's the ruler of his kingdom. Lower subjects, like cats on the floor, should know to make way for him. Hence, he's earned the title "Cat Crippler."

"Look out!" I yelled when he stepped on our kitty's paw. "Don't you *see* her?"

"Ee-ee-EE-EE-OW-OW!" the victim cried, pulling out from under his shoe.

"Now see what you've done. She's hurt," I scolded. I gave The Crippler a glare. "Don't you ever look where you're going?"

The king righted himself and solemnly replied, "You know, one day she's going to trip me right here in front of this refrigerator. I'm going to fall back into this granite countertop and crack my skull. And then, when I'm lying up in the hospital, on a respirator, with my life dangling by a thread, you'll probably lean over me and say, 'You horrible man. You injured my cat.'"

From his assessment, I think it's unwise to send hate mail to a cat person.

A Cat's Philosophy

The closer I study my cat, the more I'm sure she lives by time-tested, fool-proof principles. If she could speak, I'm pretty sure she'd tell me what her philosophy entails—right after she voiced her complaints about that earlier dog food mix-up.

As I grow older and wider, I mean *wiser*, I better appreciate my feline's behaviors. She doesn't compare herself to other cats (because she's an only pet), and she lives continuously in the present moment. If she worries at all about the future, her concerns likely extend no further than the next hair ball.

Because her vocabulary consists primarily of the words "me" and "ow," I've attempted to capture the essence of my kitty's outlook in the following credo:

A Feline's Philosophy

Approach everything new with curiosity and caution. Remain alert and prepared for change at all times. A spirit of adventure often leads to a good catch.

Keep in touch with your inner child. It's OK to kick sand or chase loose ends, now and again. Play.

Take a long nap after a big meal, and when you're feeling good—demonstrate it. Purr.

Be both a seeker and a provider of warmth. Bask in a sunny spot, if you get the chance. But remain inside whenever it's storming.

Meditate on nature.

Present a good external appearance through frequent grooming.

Help others do what they cannot do for themselves, such as lick the tops of their own heads.

Ignore what's insignificant. Bluff whenever you're unsure of yourself. Shamelessly relax any time you need or want to.

Dare to expose your underside. Your soft spots will be discovered, even if you don't.

117

Stay close to your friends.

Stretch until you've extended to your fullest reach. When uncomfortable, change positions.

It can be difficult to see well with both feet on the ground. The best views are found by climbing high.

Really, what else is there to learn?

MANAGING THE OPTICS

What's to Love About LASIK?

The number one cause of divorce after 50 is probably snoring, followed by LASIK eye surgery. And if your mate undergoes vision repair and can now see *and* hear your unattractive and annoying nocturnal honks and whistles, then either your marriage is doomed to dissolve into separate sleeping quarters or certain to attract the attention of behavioral scientists.

Now, I don't mean to suggest that corrective vision is a bad thing for anyone who needs it. But after 50, undergoing LASIK is equivalent to viewing the entire world in high definition. If you think that's healthy, just look at what HDTV has done for the careers of elder news anchors (though it's been a boon for the cosmetics industry).

Personally, I can't afford enough foundation to undergo this kind of physical scrutiny. If I had to layer on adequate makeup to hide my laugh lines, I'd no longer be able to lift my head.

You see, God made our close range vision decline after 40 for a reason. Why would anyone want to reverse this condition? Do you really want to see what's happening to your skin or observe every flaw on your partner's face? Who wants to watch crows' feet morph into ostrich legs?

I'd just as soon not view broken capillaries and runaway nose hairs unless they're on Angelina Jolie. (Yes, that was a mean shot, but we both know it'll never happen. And if it did, someone would air brush those suckers to oblivion.)

Checking the FDA website, I found a list of still more reasons why some individuals might not be good candidates for LASIK surgery. I've taken the liberty to augment this list for the sake of clarity. My additional comments appear below in bold italics.

You're Probably Not a Good Candidate for LASIK Surgery If:

- You have difficulty staring for at least 60 seconds at an object *(excluding movies starring George Clooney).*

- LASIK surgery may jeopardize your job, *marriage, or ability to ignore fine print.*

- Cost is a factor: Most medical insurance will not pay for LASIK surgery *or any resulting attorney's fees.*

- You are not a risk taker *when it comes to significant assets such as your eyes.*

- You actively participate in contact sports *or close range sex.*

- You are not an adult *past the age of 45.*

Isn't it amazing how a few words can change the entire meaning of a sentence? I hate it when government provides only partial subject information.

To the above list, I'd also add:

- **You flinch every time you attempt to apply mascara.**

- **The thought of a hot laser beam searing through your cornea makes you nauseous.**

- **You've seen the movie *Clockwork Orange.***

If you're considering LASIK surgery, please review all the risks and then, if that's not enough to deter you, try this test: Turn on an HD TV and tune the set to the *Senior Lifetime* channel. Standing at close range, observe the actors' faces. Now ask yourself this question: Is that the degree of visual clarity you wish to have when you're dining with your friends?

My guy thought he wanted to undergo LASIK eye repair but, after considering all the pros and cons, he decided against this procedure. Sometimes he'll glimpse my bare naked face and remark, "You're so beautiful." When he does this, I'm quick to remind him "love is blind." And I'm thrilled to know it's going to stay that way.

Nothing Green about Gardening

About the time our close-up vision starts to go, our inner gardener begins to emerge. Honestly, I don't understand the connection, but I suspect this need arises from a fear of eating something we can't see or recall where it came from.

Despite my age and eyesight, the gardening guru has not recruited me. And when she does, I'll be thrilled to finally have a legitimate excuse to wear some of those fancy, hand-painted, rubber clogs.

All around me, it seems that everyone is gardening. Even my daughter, who can still see fairly well and who I previously thought knew how to grow only molds, announced she's acquired some seedlings. She's attempting to grow these fragile shoots inside her high-rise apartment, one that is better suited for hosting parties than horticultural pursuits.

Having a neglected quarter acre backyard, perhaps I should be the one contemplating cultivation.

My agrarian ventures, thus far, have been confined to the nurturing of drought tolerant native plants such as purple fountain grass, lamb's ear, and mistletoe. I didn't actually introduce the mistletoe. But you get the idea.

I'm thinking that, during tough economic times like these, maybe I shouldn't let past performance influence future expectations. Possibly it's time to ignore the claims that I'm "capable of killing a cactus."

Aside from lacking any demonstrable skills, I can find many reasons not to tackle tomatoes. Sure,

I could probably grow something easy—like cucumbers. However, I don't eat cucumbers. I do love pickles. But then I'd have to solve the critical dilemma of who would make them.

Here's what really gets me about gardening; people have a tendency to grow whatever suits their soils and not their taste buds. They pay attention to superfluous stuff, such as climate, rather than to what they might actually enjoy consuming. Otherwise, we'd witness more tobacco gardens, backyard vineyards, and cocoa orchards. Not to mention *illegal* crops, which I most assuredly *don't* condone.

My point is this: If I'm going to have to water and weed a garden, then it had better be producing something I'll use—besides another excuse to avoid housework.

Currently, I spend about $4 per week for tomatoes, $4 for lettuce, and another $6 or so for other miscellaneous vegetables. Multiply that by 50 (because I vacation at least 2 weeks every year) and the result would be barely enough cost savings to buy the extra refrigerator I'd need to store all the red globes and greens a garden would supply.

If I planted a 12-foot by 20-foot patch of produce, I'd need an extra freezer, a roadside vegetable stand, or a lot more friends who cook to handle my harvests. Any added appliances would pull even more electricity than I'm already using. This might benefit employment because the increase could spur construction of a new power plant. But it would be terrible for my budget, if I actually had one.

All the outdoor labor required to maintain a garden would cause me to do something I seldom do now: sweat. I've said this before, but it bears repeating. Every time I perspire, I develop a bad attitude.

Once I grew moist and musty, I'd need more energy to heat the water for extra showers. This, in turn, would lead me to launder more towels, which would cause my dryer to further heat my house in the summertime, and that would trigger my air conditioner to run even harder than it might otherwise.

The additional laundry loads would force me to buy more detergent packaged in plastic petroleum-based containers that are manufactured out of state, trucked cross-country, and sold to folks like me who drive their cars several miles to acquire it.

So how, I ask, can gardening be "green?"

If I really want to be helpful, healthy, and hospitable, I should simply accept the overages my friends are surely going to be retrieving from their gardens. From the looks of their current efforts, I'm still going to need an extra refrigerator.

High Food Costs Make Me Creative

During The Great Recession, that might or might not be over, depending on whether you do or don't believe in fairy tales, many families have ceased dining out. Where are these folks buying their groceries?

The only way I could cook a burger and fries for less than McDonald's will serve me a combo meal would be to skip the bun, hold the produce, and ignore the grease fire.

With grocery and gas prices spiraling the way they are now, I can afford to either drive to the store or shop—but not both. I'm thinking of posting a bumper sticker on my car that reads "Will Walk for Food!"

Electricity is a concern when cooking at home too. Every time I turn on a burner or fire up the oven, I might as well throw an imported chocolate bar out the window. Seldom does one make it past my lips (or hips). So it should be obvious that I'm speaking metaphorically.

Some suggest we should eat foods produced closer to home. If I were to do that, my diet would consist of rabbit stew, grackle pie, and lawn clover salad garnished with hackberries.

To help reduce the cost of dining in, this year, our family's Memorial Day cookout will be B.Y.O.C. (bring your own chips). Yes, with the rising cost of corn- and wheat-based products, we simply have to resort to drastic measures.

Instead of slow-cooking my brisket on our gas grill, this holiday I'm going to park the car in a sunny spot, raise the windows, and set the beef in a glass casserole dish underneath the rear window. In the floorboard, I'll brew a pitcher of sun tea. (Remember, I live in the Southwest.) I'll steam the potatoes inside storage baggies in my dishwasher while running a load of dishes. Or perhaps I'll just toss them in the dryer with a load of towels. One cannot think too creatively during an economic crisis.

We'll skip the corn on the cob this season. It's become too scarce a commodity, thanks to the discovery and promotion of ethanol. And besides, people are bicycling in China.

Speaking of the Orient, which I'm fairly certain is where China is located, I heard there might be a rice shortage too. However, I haven't eaten white rice since I found out it sticks to my thighs.

All this havoc at the markets has hampered my weight loss plans. I'd hoped to lose a few pounds before vacation time, and that necessitates a low-carb diet of lean meats, low-fat dairy products, fruits, and vegetables. Come on. Who am I kidding? If I could afford to eat like that, I wouldn't *have* to. I could pay for liposuction.

No, for once, I'm looking at my extra heft with newfound confidence. Though I may not be rich or thin, physically, I'm recession-proof.

MP3 & QVC Madness

The most embarrassing item my husband has ever purchased is a portable MP3 player. That probably sounds like a rather innocuous device, but this music storage unit has turned my spouse, for the *second* time in his life, into a "headbanger."

The tunes of his past have arrived to claim my 55-year-old travel companion, causing him to lose all regard for propriety. As I write this, I am seated next to him, inside an airplane, and there is no place for me to hide. He reads the newspaper and violently nods to some beat that thankfully remains inaudible to those nearby. In what appears to be a moment of sheer audio bliss, he whips out an ear pod and shoves it, without warning, into my own hearing orifice. Instantly I recognize the tune, a Pink Floyd classic hit.

Ever so casually I note that he is reading the financial section of the newspaper while listening to the song, "Money." I consider pointing this out before I realize he's on such a mental excursion there's little use. Only seconds ago, I looked over and caught him, I swear to Black Sabbath, playing air guitar!

He is purposefully trying to annoy me, break my concentration, or send me into a shame spiral. And it's working.

I do my best to pretend that I don't know him—which is rather difficult to pull off, considering that every once in a while he gives me a look that suggests he's conducting a private concert for my benefit. His face contorts, eyes squint tight. Then he whispers a bad-boy "Yeah!" and studies me for signs of reaction.

135

If I were a less modest person, I'd flash him, so help me ZZ Top, with a raised T-shirt. I'd maybe follow that with a little not-so-private seat dance to further humiliate him. But he knows I grew up crooning to bubble gum music, so it's no secret that I lack the guts to be this vulgar.

There must have been a song shuffle because now he's a keyboardist, frantically playing "The William Tell Overture." I entertain thoughts of slamming his airline tray table on his acrobatic fingers, anything to rock him back to American Airlines Coach Class. But he is too far gone for even that to gain his attention.

Relief comes only when he periodically checks his breast pocket. That's where the menacing music machine is located. From all appearances, you'd think he'd detected an irregular, maybe even fatal, pulse. He makes a quick adjustment and then returns to Starship Nine or wherever the heck he imagines himself.

As I have the window seat, I am a captive audience to his clowning. I always seem to play the straight one to his goofiness, which, in all honesty, is why I write humor. Seldom do I get the chance to be funny at home because he's already claimed that role.

When I'd initially selected this airplane seat, I'd hoped to prepare for an interview scheduled for tomorrow. I have a list to review, and one of the questions I'm supposed to answer is "Who's the funniest person you know?".

I stare at the heavy-metal listener seated next to me and find my answer bobbing his head.

I Shouldn't Have Left Him Home Alone with the Remote

My first mistake was hinting that I wanted an upright freezer. My second was leaving my husband home, alone, bored and recovering from spine surgery.

"I might as well tell you," he confessed, "I did something bad while you were gone."

Visions of 65-inch TV screens and credit card bills large enough to threaten our mortgage payment danced through my mind.

"What?" I gripped the kitchen countertop for extra support.

"You know how you said you were planning to get a freezer?"

"I didn't say I was 'planning' to get one," I corrected. "I just said I needed more freezer space and wanted to price a few."

"Yeah, well, anyway, I figured you were serious about getting one, so I bought us something to go in it!" hubby exclaimed.

"I already have something to go in it . . . the overflow from the existing one," I reminded.

"Oh, wait until you see the steaks I bought!" said my mystery shopper. "They're awesome. Not the crappy kind you've been getting from the grocery store, either. These are big and juicy and taste wonderful!"

"Someone came to our door offering steak samples?" *Man, the economy must be worse than I'd thought.*

"No. But I *saw* them."

"Huh? Where?"

He ducked his head low and peered up at me. "On QVC."

"You bought *meat* off the TV?" I gasped. "Please tell me you're kidding."

"Hon, they are going to be SOOOOO good."

"How do you *know?*"

"Because I SAW them!"

"And you think you viewed the actual steaks you're going to receive?"

Hubby shrugged.

I jaunted to our side-by-side unit and, because I wasn't wearing hard-toe shoes, gingerly opened the freezer door. With one hand, I rubbed at my forehead and counted to . . . well . . . at least two.

"When are these steaks supposed to arrive?"

"Soon," he said.

"How soon?"

If I threw away the ice cream bucket wedged between the pizza and the burgers I hadn't yet compared to the most recent recall list, maybe I could make room for a sirloin or two. That leftover ice ring of frozen fruit would probably not be needed unless I planned to throw a recovery party. And if those twice baked, three-year-old potatoes hadn't yet made their way to our dining table, they probably never would.

"I don't know," said my chronic channel surfer.

"Have you looked in here?" I motioned to the refrigerator. Then I remembered he'd been eating mostly soft foods and taking pain meds. "OK," I said, faking renewed calm. "Just tell me exactly how many steaks you ordered. Four? Six? Eight?"

Seconds passed before he answered, "Twenty-four."

I'm not sure where we're heading with health care reform, but I'm going to need family medical insurance that offers QVC protection.

How to Speak So That Your Spouse Will Listen

For perfectly legitimate reasons, I seldom talk to my spouse about his job. Whenever I ask about his work, he typically answers me in some unintelligible language.

"How was your day?" I'll inquire.

Then he'll set down his laptop computer bag, sigh, and say something like, "The AVPs for the UMZ and PSVN units were in town, so I had to give an OMB presentation to the ISBQ staff."

Then my eyes start to droop and I snap back to attention just long enough to reply, "Oh," before I return to watching the *Evening Snooze*.

If I have to stop an individual after every four words to ask him to explain an acronym, I figure the subject is wholly unworthy of conversation. Communicating with my husband about business is like talking to a teen about pop culture. Our terminologies are too vastly different to endure the pain.

I'm not, and don't wish to become, fluent in industry jargon. Nonetheless, I've picked up a few *Corporatease* terms and definitions by accident. On the outside chance that you might need them when attempting conversation with your significant other, here they are:

Global firm – a company that can, and most likely will, eventually transfer your job overseas.

IT – an acronym for the department that deals with geek-related gobbly-gook that nobody else can or wants to understand.

Systems integration – a synonym for "computer anarchy."

Major conversion – an event that causes customers to rage and employees to work weekends.

Cross-pollinate – a nice way of saying "your travel demands are about to triple."

Reduce expenses – a phrase used to notify workers that the break room brewed coffee has just been eliminated and all paper towels must henceforth be brought from home. (Note: This will in no way reduce executive management bonuses.)

Right-sized – an alert that signals a pending layoff and infers the company has gotten too big for its cubicles.

Outsourced – what the company does with your job when they find someone in another country who's willing to take even greater abuse than you do for less money than you're paid.

Non-performers – the 80 percent of staff whom, for ambiguous reasons, will not be laid off (see "outsourced" and "right-sized") and yet will not qualify for an annual performance raise.

Career mobility – a human resource term that indicates the only opportunities for advancement exist outside the firm.

Managing the optics – what your boss says when he or she wants to hide the fact that you're doing his or her work.

Value added – the amount of profits the company makes as a result of underpaying you for your services.

Stakeholders – anyone whose interest in a corporate endeavor would cause them to, should that endeavor fail, feel compelled to drive a stake through the responsible party's heart.

Draconian efforts – any work process which does not conform to the existing corporate culture, such as paying attention to details.

If you should need more definitions like these, I highly suggest finding someone else to talk to.

Running From Local Office

Every home, corporate, or civic environment has its own customs and languages, and city hall is no exception. Typically, there's some written code of conduct or general understanding—and then there's reality. Here's a hypothetical example: All city hiring will be based solely on individual qualifications. Coincidentally, the most qualified candidate for the last job was a guy who happens to be dating the daughter of the police chief whose wife's brother owns the local Quickie-Mart and the brother's wife chairs city council.

I believe you can learn a great deal about a community by counting the number of people campaigning for local offices. A high number of candidates could indicate a low level of public awareness.

Holding elected or appointed city positions equates to serving an honorable civic duty for which volunteers are handsomely repaid by loss of friendships, leisure activities, and, above all, brain cells.

It all begins with *Robert's Rules of Order*, a set of parliamentary procedures that are frequently referenced though rarely followed.

Army Brigadier General Henry Robert wrote "The Rules" after he failed to successfully chair a gathering at his local Baptist church. Why we use these guidelines in government remains a mystery to me. If you've ever been to a town hall meeting, you know the vocal residents who attend these events aren't exactly looking for religion. They're there to find either justice or a news camera.

Though often rowdy, local government meetings are best described as public assemblies wherein many motions—yet few advances—are made. I know this from experience because I once served a two-year term on a planning and zoning commission. This naturally only gave residents another reason to laugh at their local officials.

While on public watch, I deliberated over such pressing issues as revisions to a city fence ordinance and changes to subdivision regulations for driveway construction. Valliant efforts were undertaken during public meetings. I can truthfully report that, not once, despite overwhelming urges, did I ever, even after both audience members had nodded off, lose consciousness.

Our commission determined that wood slats, stone masonry, and wrought iron were suitable fencing materials—and that barbed wire, broken solar panels, and mobile home skirting were not. Furthermore, we concluded that every home should have a driveway, and some of them could be shaped like a "J." Previously, this consonant had been stigmatized and discriminated against.

These decisions were forwarded to City Council for final approval, which, I'm happy to say, was obtained without triggering a council weekend workshop in Las Vegas.

When a city council makes a decision, i.e. when an agenda item can no longer be rescheduled, authorization for action is issued by a formal resolution, a document that reads something like this:

WHEREAS, nobody at City Hall has a clue as to what might be the current zoning for XYZ property ("The Property"); and,

WHEREAS, the owner of The Property ("Owner") stands to make a killing if The Property is zoned for use as a beer store; and,

WHEREAS, Owner agrees to dedicate 1/100 of The Property to the City if The Property is zoned for use as a beer store; and,

WHEREAS, the City needs the said 1/100 of The Property to correct a roadway misalignment that recently sent a car careening into a dwelling; and,

WHEREAS, Owner has threatened to sue for an amount equivalent to ten times the annual City budget if Owner's property zoning request is denied; therefore, be it

RESOLVED, that The Property shall be zoned for use as a beer store.

Participating in local government can be extremely educational. *

* A special note from my attorney: Statements contained herein are purely satirical. Any similarities to real people, places, or events are wholly coincidental though not entirely surprising.

How to Invest During a Recession

As we enter our later earning years, it's natural to become more focused on savings and investments. No, I'm not referring to vintage doll and baseball card collections. Yes, I know these are currently worth more than the securities in your retirement account. But that's not my point. Don't worry about past losses. You can always delay retirement until your children are sufficiently well off to take care of you.

The first thing you should do to protect any remaining assets is cancel any and all subscriptions to investment newsletters. Why? Well, did any of these geniuses tell you to sell your stocks before the bear market set in? I didn't think so. There's no reason to continue paying for investment advice. You can do just as well, if not better, by following your horoscope.

The next action you'll want to take deals with your employer (assuming you still have one). Do you receive earnings alerts and corporate updates about company stock? I bet so did Enron employees. And we know how well that worked out for them. Any time your employer conducts an emotionally-charged, upbeat earnings conference call, you should short the stock.

While I'm on the subject of stocks, my best suggestion would be to avoid these securities in favor of buying garden seed. At least that can sow something more than corporate greed.

It makes sense to diversify your investments. This, naturally, means you'll need to establish an eBay account.

When it comes to real estate, consider buying apartment futures.

I've no idea what to advise you about oil and gas. That ship has already left the Middle East, if you catch my wave. Otherwise, I'd recommend purchasing a refinery.

My thoughts about bonds are simple: you should refrain, if at all possible, from ever having to post one.

What about gold? All I can say is this: Now who's stupid for installing those over-the-top bathroom fixtures? Remember the gals you called idiots for wearing jewelry fashioned from Krugerrands? Some fads turn out to be prophetic.

Finally, I have to admit I don't understand the appeal of insurance and annuities. Why would you want to wager a bet in which other parties win if you die? That's seems self-explanatory, so I won't elaborate any further. Besides, Guido The Actuary and I have an agreement.

If All Else Fails, Become a Bank

Having observed the events of the past few years, I've decided the best way to recover from The Great Recession is to become a bank. Thus, I've composed the following letter to the Federal Reserve:

Dear Federal Reserve:

Please consider this letter as my formal request to become a bank holding company. Yes, I know I'm a proprietor with too many liabilities and not enough assets. But the way I've got it figured, that makes me no different than any other entity you've so generously approved for bank conversion.

If American Express can become a bank, then why can't I? I loan money too. OK, so what if that's just to my kids?

When I don't get paid back, then I'm in jeopardy of defaulting on my debt obligations.

Therefore, I need some deposits (other than those being left on my lawn by rude dogs). What I need is a government cash infusion, and I'm not talking about one of those pathetic stimulus checks that won't even cover the cost of a decent holiday bash, minus a DJ.

If I were a bank, I could make promises to my shareholders, depositors, and employees that I wouldn't have to keep unless I felt like it. I could say "no" to anyone I pleased without fear of ever having those tables turned on me. And I could carelessly risk others' savings instead of my own hard IOUs.

If I were a bank, I could receive billions from the government in return for devalued assets—like, say, maybe my house—that no one else would want. I could borrow money at less than one percent and loan those same funds to A-credit borrowers at pawn shop rates. It would be SWEET! And all the while, I could feel magnanimous about the services I'm providing for individuals and businesses, ones that either are less fortunate or suffer from inadequate lobbyists and inferior legal counsel.

I could run giant ads in major newspapers to boast about the community good will I'm providing. And no one would look further to see how many US jobs I'm continuing to transfer overseas.

If you'd just permit me to become a bank, I could save myself from the utter ravages of this collapsing economy—and from something even more frightening and potentially fatal: consequences.

Managing Financial Stress

Financial uncertainty can raise anxiety levels. Though there's no way to predict the future, I've been told the practice of meditation can help minimize fears and worries. Meditation has been known to reduce the effects of all types of tension, except pants seam stress. For that, I'd have to add fasting.

This morning, I thought I'd give meditation a try. So I sat down in the comfort of my reading room, surrounded by magazine litter, disorganized books, and other clutter, and attempted to become One with The Universe.

Who ever knew birds could be so loud? They wouldn't stop chirping so I could hear that Still Small Voice within. So I started chanting, silently, to distract myself from the shrill singing and the percussion of pounding hammers. (Someone is building a home two blocks from my house.)

I am grateful for this day. I give thanks for all that I've received. I ask only that You guide me in the direction of my highest good.

Chee-ee-urp! Chee-ee-urp! Chee-ee-urp-urp-urp.

Whack, whack, whack!

OK. This isn't working.

Wait a minute. What did Eckhart Tolle say in his book, *The Power of Now*? Or was it *A New Earth*? You know, about the spaces between thoughts? Oh, yeah. I'm supposed to try and extend the time between my thoughts so that the intervals become longer and longer.

I will think no thoughts.

(pause)

But isn't "I will think no thoughts" a thought? Oh, great. I've already botched it.

Seriously. That's it. No more thoughts. Not a single one.

(Moments pass.)

I did it! I didn't think a single thing for, what? At least several seconds. Uh-huh, but now here I am THINKING about how long I've managed to not think! I've probably negated the benefits of whatever minor accomplishments I've made.

This is insane.

Try again.

I entertain nothing but the quietness within me.

You ninny! That was a thought!

Start over.

"Start over" was a thought!

Stop, already! Quit thinking! Let it go-o-o. Just be.

Time and external stimuli ceased.

And then I woke up.

Did that count?

HOLLYWOOD HAZARDS

Why Men Like Explosions in Movies

Several friends and I recently discussed the differences between men's and women's tastes in movies. I'm talking about action adventures compared to life dramas that deal with more realistic subjects, such as finding a soul mate via time travel.

Guys want the movies they watch to be packed with astonishing pyrotechnics that deliver excessive jolts of adrenaline.

"If something doesn't blow up in the first 15 minutes," my friend's spouse confessed, "I'm out of there."

The other men seated at our restaurant table nodded in agreement.

We ladies shared a knowing laugh.

Then one of the kitchen's wait staff dropped what sounded like a four-piece serving for 50. The gentleman seated next to me expressed his concerns by applauding.

Why are men so enamored with things that go "BANG?" I wondered.

Perhaps the male of our species welcomes anything that interrupts otherwise constant thoughts of sex.

Nah, that can't be it. Nothing could be *that* jarring.

When it comes to movies, men are attracted to explosions and fires and guns because viewing these images of power helps satisfy their urges to destroy opposition.

Think you won that last argument with your man? Nope. He obliterated your score while watching *Transformers*. You just didn't know it.

Gals, here's the deal: Men are wired to want something to erupt—loudly. This clearly works to their advantage. As long as there's plenty of noise, they can avoid listening to us *talk*.

Furthermore, car explosions and artillery bombs and asteroid collisions boost men's confidence because they're always looking for an equalizer to prove size *really* doesn't matter. They've never been fully convinced.

The metaphorical links between explosions and heated desires have been well established. Items that can be detonated are dangerous, and danger, as everyone knows, is an aphrodisiac. This explains why many men say they're "looking for fireworks in the bedroom."

Explosives are naturally arousing. Good grief, the word "combustible" even includes the word "bust."

To a guy, there's nothing more thrilling than giant fireballs spewing debris and carnage. Don't ask them to watch a movie that has a dramatic plot, one with actual dialogue and fully clothed stars. That would require too much cerebral effort for anything that lacks a powerful climax.

However, when I'm watching a movie, if something blows up during the first 15 minutes, then I expect whatever follows to be a two-hour waste. Unless, of course, that is the inciting incident that sends the heroine on a journey of self-discovery that takes her to some exotic locale, wherein she meets some gorgeous hunk of hormones who is suffering from a tragic loss, and they fall in love, drift apart, and then, through some chance event, reunite and eventually marry and live harmoniously ever after, despite having four children, three dogs, two cats, one iguana, and a mother-in-law sharing their quarters.

See, women are just more realistic when it comes to what they expect from movies.

Blazing Brisket

It's not that unusual to look out my kitchen windows and see flames. Especially when my husband is grilling. But when I realized a fire was leaping three-feet above the grill vents, I said, "Hubby, we have a problem."

At that moment, the cook was standing indoors, eyes transfixed on the television screen. Susan Sarandon was saying something to Geena Davis, so my alert didn't fully register.

"The grill is on FIRE!" I shouted.

He glanced outside and then sauntered through the back door. "It's just a little grease," he reassured. "It always does this."

My distracted mate had been partially right. However, I normally don't ask him to sear a brisket the size of my thighs. (Yes, both of them). There'd been enough fat on that hunk of beef to fuel an all-night campfire.

His instructions had been to simply brown the meat on both sides and then return the brisket to me for slow cooking. The number of elapsed minutes since he'd become enthralled with *Thelma & Louise* remains a mystery. He said maybe five. I'm thinking more like, 15.

My backyard broil master turned off the gas. Then, against my better advice, he grabbed a long-handle spatula and raised the grill lid.

Fire lurched out in all directions.

He dropped the cover and jumped back.

"Whoa," he said, which I immediately understood as the universal *man code* for "I've no friggin' idea what to do."

"I'll get the fire extinguisher," I hollered.

"Noooo! Don't you dare."

"Why not?"

"Because you'll *ruin* the brisket," he insisted.

Now, to appreciate the credibility of that statement, let me fully describe the scene: Flames spiraled near the wood beams supporting our patio roof. Blazes licked the grill front, near the knobs. A steady wind whipped through an air vent on one side of the cooker, breathing what looked like a blow torch flame out the opposite side vent. Despite a lack of propane, the inferno was growing more powerful by the minute.

"Ohmigod," I screamed. "The PROPANE TANK! You've got to get it out of there! It could blow! Get it out! Getitout! GETITOUT!!"

My now present-minded spouse unhooked the connections and pulled the tank free.

I grabbed the cylinder and hauled it another 30 feet farther from where he'd set it, just to be sure.

"We'll snuff it out," hubby said of the fire. "Hold this pan against the vents with this." He handed me a grill cleaning implement made of thick rubber. Yeah. Good call.

I did as he'd instructed, but soon the implement melted and an odiferous burning tire-scented smoke overtook me.

"That's it," I said, "I'm calling the fire department."

"NO. Don't call them. It's just a grease fire. It'll burn out."

I stood there, considering his directive. And then the knobs on the front of the grill melted and fell off.

"I'M CALLING THE FIRE DEPARTMENT. Before we burn the house down!"

The first people on the scene were the police and ambulance. Unless the paramedics were trained to treat embarrassment, I'm not sure what they'd plan to do.

By the time the fire truck arrived with its crew, the grill was completely destroyed but the blaze had grown considerably smaller. A cluster of fully suited firemen hurried into the backyard and stood ready for action. There they met my exasperated husband, grill side.

After much laughter, one of the firemen said, "Well, let's open it up and see what we've got left."

On the grate set a perfectly unidentifiable smoldering slab of meat, one that was now about a third of its original mass.

"Man, that's a shame," said the fireman, "because I was really hungry."

Once the public servants left, my spouse looked disapprovingly at me and said, "I TOLD you not to call them."

"We tried to fight that fire for over 20 minutes," I whined. "How was I to know when it was going to burn out?" I stared at the remains of the family dinner main course I'd planned to serve the next day. I'd need to make another grocery store run, for sure.

"Oh, no," said hubby. "I'm not throwing this away. Not after all that. Nuh-uh. We're EATING *this* brisket."

"No way."

"Yep. I'll just scrape off the burned part."

"Burned part?" I stared at him in disbelief. "That brisket was on fire for a *half-hour*. It's a cremated calf! I'm not serving that to anybody."

I left him paying his last respects to the charcoaled carcass and went in search of a replacement.

When I arrived home, my determined and quite possibly deranged partner already had trimmed the black off the burned brisket. He'd ruined my best cookie tray in the process (though he blamed the fire) and had transferred soot to parts of the floor and most of my kitchen countertops.

He stood there, with flecks of incinerated beef clinging to his shirt, hands, and even the hairs on his arms, as he triumphantly announced, "Look. It's still pink inside."

The room smelled like a barn fire, and he exhibited the appearance and mental acumen of a dazed survivor.

"I am not cooking that brisket. It's destroyed. Give it up. I bought a new one."

Hubby acted like he didn't hear me, despite the absence of Susan Sarandon.

For the next four hours, we held a cook-off. My brisket slow roasted in the oven, smelling all barbecue-like and sweet, while his simmered in a crock pot, stinking up the whole house.

Every time I lifted the crock pot lid, the meat smelled worse. "This isn't getting any better, you know," I observed.

"It'll be fine. It just needs some sauce," he replied.

At midnight, I cut up my brisket and stowed it away for the next day's family meal. Hubby sampled my tender dish and then took a bite of his own doings.

His eyes met mine.

"Told 'ya," I said as sympathetically as possible.

He tossed six hours of labor into the trash and sighed.

Fantasies can be terribly hard to let go.

Why I'm Not an Actor

I'd grown bored and was looking for a new challenge when I signed up for an intensive half-day acting workshop that I felt sure would help me to sound like Diane Sawyer. Or if not, at least better than Miss Piggy.

The instructor, a woman who happens to be related to a well-known Hollywood star, began with a discussion about "parking." I'd thought I was finished with that subject about 30 years ago. But as it turned out, she was referring to where a person should place his or her hands while *speaking*. Apparently, over your crotch is inadvisable—unless you're communicating with rappers.

After a little more instruction, it was time to put what participants had learned to use. Each of us was given a commercial script to memorize and perform on camera. My role was to be the company spokesperson for a pharmacy (which seemed highly improbable though strangely suitable, given my profession).

I was to convey the message that my firm sincerely cared about providing personal service. Now, I ask you, when was the last time your pharmacy sent you a birthday card? Uh-huh. I thought so. And don't tell me they don't have the date.

Ignoring this apparent conflict, I forged ahead . . . after I stopped editing the copy. I couldn't help myself. When I noticed the noun "effect" substituted for the verb "affect," I whipped out my pen and made the correction. I managed to stop short of underlining the vague pronoun references and improper punctuation. No one had asked me to perform copy editing services. My job was to push product, promote an image, and generally prove my talent for lying. At least one of those skills I'd already mastered.

"We're here for your health," was my opening line. As I parted my lips to speak, I heard an inner voice asking, whom, exactly, are "we?" I was the only one in the scene. Granted, over the holidays I'd gained a few pounds. Maybe five. All right, exactly eight, if you must know. But that didn't qualify me to be spoken of in plural form.

Where was "here?" Was this a direct reference to some physical location or simply vernacular, as in "I'm here for you."? And how can I exist *for* someone else's health? That is, unless that individual is a cannibal.

"Stop," said my instructor. "You're not being you. You're giving us who you think we want to see and not who you really are."

Yes, but right then the *real* me was preoccupied with what I call my "infernal editor." I felt sure no one in the room would understand this.

I can't help it. I'm possessed with an over-analyzing, super-critical, perfection-seeking inner demon that torments me when I read copy. The only time this voice goes away is when I'm reviewing my own work.

The next bit of dialogue was, "That's why we're specializing in . . . ."

There was that "we" again! Ahhhh! We whom? The company? The pharmacists? The minimum wage-earning clerks selling toiletries and breath mints? And why not just say "we specialize in" instead of "we're specializ*ing* in?" Maybe the firm is still evolving. Has the business not yet become fully specialized? Are they (whomever "they" might be) still seeking some type of specialized certification? I don't want to do business with a pharmacy that isn't completely up to par.

"Uh-huh," my coach admonished. "You're doing it again."

Indeed.

I struggled on, attempting to sound believable. But when I arrived at the part that said, "Your pharmacist is trained in allergy relief . . . ," I started laughing. How can a pharmacist be "trained in allergy relief?" He or she can be trained to dispense advice about symptom relief or to suggest medications that might help allergy symptoms. But if you have allergies, you have them. (I'm a lifelong sufferer.) There isn't any such thing as allergy relief, short of a complicated course that involves doctors' visits and enough needle punctures to leave you looking like you've been wrestling porcupines.

Someone recently told me about oil of oregano, which works better for allergy symptoms than anything I've tried to date. However, I doubt your pharmacist will ever mention *that* treatment. Just know that when you use this potent natural remedy, the oil may leave you smelling like a pizzeria. Good for allergies. Bad for dieters. **

"Look," said my acting coach. "Just be YOU."

She had no idea what she was asking.

I've been writing far too long to know how to act.

*** Important Medical Disclaimer: I am neither trained nor qualified to offer medical advice. In fact, I'm not really qualified to offer ANY advice, so consult your common sense before following any of my recommendations.*

College Acting Class, Day 1: Freezing My A@# Off

After that brief acting workshop, I decided maybe I needed a full semester of acting classes, so I signed up for a couple courses at the junior college near my home. A friend encouraged me to take these classes with her. Although I seldom need much prompting to try something new—unless that's a man, and then I'm sticking with the brand I've come to trust if not obey.

Colleges and universities are familiar territories to me. But I can honestly say this was the first time I'd ever heard an instructor refer to students as "f_ _ ers." So right off, I could see there would be a language barrier.

What I also discovered is that normal classes meet in standard classrooms, the kind where there's sufficient lighting and heat in the winter. But *acting* classes meet in large stage areas and auditoriums where, apparently, administration only turns on the heat for paying ticket holders. When an instructor shows up wearing a down-filled parka, three layers of clothing, and a winter neck scarf, it's never a good sign. In fact, I'd call that "foreshadowing."

In my diction course, I was told to purchase a yoga mat and to wear workout clothing and athletic shoes to class. I had no idea that speaking could be this strenuous.

181

Day 2: I'm Going to Need More Memory

Today I have learned how to combine silly sounds with pointless gestures—all, of course, in fluid form. I have also discovered how to cross a room, repeatedly, while dodging 18 other men and women who seem intent on vying for my space. I have breathed while making eye contact, at close range, with strangers. And I have stretched my body and then let it become small, or at least as small as I can shrink a size 12.

After my instructor asked me to, off the cuff, recite some verse or prose, being the learned writer that I am, I came up with, "I promise to love God and my country, to help other people everywhere, especially those at home." What was that? My Girl Scout oath? I don't even know where that came from! Obviously, I didn't want to use this. Eventually I managed to pull a bunny out of my bonnet. I recited a quote from *The Velveteen Rabbit*, by Margery Williams.

So far, other than the spontaneous recitation, it feels like I'm back in kindergarten. My first homework assignment is to pore over several classic American plays and find a monologue that is "most like me." I will then have to memorize and perform these lines before the class. I feel like Mary Katherine Gallagher of *Saturday Night Live* fame. "My feelings would be best expressed in a monologue . . . ."

Day 3: Breathing Thru My Vagina

If you've ever seen that MAD TV skit with Michael McDonald, the one where he played the part of a yoga instructor, you have some idea of what yesterday's diction class was like. In the episode I just referred to, McDonald's character is telling a class full of women to imagine that they are breathing through their vaginas.

Here we all were, lying on our little mats, with our buttocks in the air, when the instructor said, "Now imagine breathing through your whole body, through every opening." And I got that mental image I just mentioned.

A convulsing spasm spiraled up from my gut. If I'd let it out, I felt pretty sure I would roll into a fit of hysterical cackling. Clamping my hands over my mouth, I held tight.

I will not laugh. I will not laugh. I will NOT burst out laughing.

Somehow, I managed to stifle the urge.

But then we were told to lie on our backs and inhale deeply, then exhale with vocalization (a sigh and then a hum). Because the class is comprised of both men and women, the noises released spanned multiple octaves. Groans escaped students at random intervals. As I tried to concentrate on what might be my signature sound, it occurred to me that what I was hearing easily could have been mistaken for a pod of whales. And with my caboose in the air, there may have been other resemblances. Again, I did my best to keep my composure . . . or as much composure as a gal can have while assuming what I call "the gynecological pose."

Standing upright, I had no better success. From my "center," I was supposed to imagine a glowing point of light. (I thought of ET, here.) With that light, I was further instructed to, I'm not kidding, "paint the wall" in front of me. This, mind you, was the same wall with which I'd already become intimately familiar because I'd previously been told to share my memorized monologue with the concrete blocks.

If I can just manage my giggle response, I should advance quickly in this class because I'm already skilled at talking to walls. After all, I've been married for 20 years.

Day 4: Good Students Don't Have Big Boobs

I'm going to get thrown out of my diction class if I don't stop laughing. What the (bleep) is wrong with me? I can't quit having insanely funny images and thoughts when I'm supposed to be serious. Nobody else in my group has this problem. Just me. I'm beginning to think maybe I'm horribly maladjusted. (No response required here.) But then, if I am, I suppose acting class is the right place for me.

During one exercise, our class was told to sit up straight with our legs underneath our buttocks and, beginning at our collarbones, walk our fingers along our sternums.

My instructor, who's male, demonstrates. His fingers drum along the center of his chest, moving gradually down to where his ribs end. I follow along, feeling the first few contact points. But then I lose touch, entirely. Something is in the way. What the heck is *that*? Oh, yeah, BOOBS!

So while all the guys in the class are fingertip dancing with their sternums, I'm over here trying to pry through the mass of flesh underneath my shelf bra—doing my best to separate what has been compressed into a doughy blob. Unlike Playtex brassieres, sports bras purchased at Target apparently don't "lift and separate."

I can't help it. I'm snickering. Now giggling.

Mr. Sternum Finder stops, looks at me, and says, "Did you hit your tickle button?"

I'm DYING to say, "No. I hit my UNIBOOB!" But I refrain. And you know, the mere thought just makes me laugh harder.

Is there a cure for this? Yes. It's called "drop this class."

My Bad Duck Audition

Admittedly, I hadn't done my homework before naively walking into my first stage audition. I'd rehearsed my lines for an entire afternoon. Or for at least a couple hours between checking my email, watching Oprah, and cooking dinner. My objective wasn't so much to land a part as it was to experience the mortification of the audition process.

To that end, I'd have to say that I brilliantly succeeded.

Having skipped (or been wrongly permitted to advance past) Acting I, I didn't know the first cardinal rule of auditions: Never look right at the auditors. So I stared straight into the director's face and began delivering my lines. She, in turn, offered her best imitation of a TSA (Transportation Security Administration) agent. This rattled me so much that I completely lost all memory and had to start over—at which point I was advised to "look at the empty theater seats."

What a relief! The vacant chairs seemed so much friendlier.

My monologue had been lifted right out of a book I'd ordered online and had received only the day before. Set sometime in the early 1900s, this British play's dialogue seemed awkward. In particular, one part appeared to make no sense at all. However, I didn't question word choices because

I imagined these sentences contained foreign idioms. I just delivered the lines as written.

At the end of my audition, the director said, "Did you know you said, 'We were dogged by bad *duck* from beginning to end'?"

I shook my head, indicating yes. Perhaps I'd mispronounced the word "dogged" and had left off the second syllable. "Did I say 'dog-ged'?" I asked.

"Yes, you said 'dog-ged' correctly," said the casting director. Biting her lips, she paused before continuing. "But did you realize you said you were dogged by bad DUCK?" The heretofore expressionless woman snickered, revealing the first hint of personality.

"Well, yes," I explained. "That's what it said in my book . . . and you know, now that you mention it, I wondered about that. Please tell me my book doesn't contain a typo. Was the word supposed to be "luck?"

Now shamelessly giggling, the director said, "Yes, the word is LUCK." When she'd regained her composure, she added," I had this image of you being chased all over Europe by vicious ducks . . . and little crosswalk signs that said 'Beware: Mean ducks.'"

I didn't get the part, but I proved I can still make 'em laugh.

HOLIDAY SURVIVAL SKILLS

Skipping Halloween

It's not considered neighborly, but I'd prefer to skip trick-or-treating and let the stores hand out my candy. I mean, the goods are already there. The way we're doing it now seems like a pretty inefficient means of distribution. I buy the candy from the grocer, haul it home, dump it in a large container, and then wait for other people to drive their children across town, to my house, where they ring my doorbell and threaten to act out if I don't give them the treats.

How about this, instead: I pay the store $20 and they hand out $100 worth of candy, since $20 is their actual cost? This way, my money goes further, they generate more store traffic, and I get to remain in my recliner.

Really, it's difficult for me to support a holiday that promotes tooth decay, egg misuse, and addictions like chocoholism. If I had my way, I'd turn off the lights, switch my doorbell breaker to the "off" position, and forget Halloween altogether.

My problem with this observance is that it teaches children one of their earliest lessons in entitlement. They learn, sometimes before they're even a year old, that by looking cute they can demand what they want from adults. Oh, sure, you're probably thinking "But it's just Tootsie Rolls." Yes, but soon enough their solicitations advance to Barbie dolls and riding toys. And before you know it, the ingrates are expecting new Toyotas for their 16th birthdays.

For the record, I wasn't raised to think I was owed anything.

When I was a youngster, my daddy said, "You want an allowance? OK. Today, I'm *allowing* you to eat. And tonight, I'm *allowing* you to sleep here too!"

If you ask me, and actually, I'll tell you even if you don't, we should encourage youth to be more resourceful and less troublesome. We need more individuals who think like the young man in Canada who recently discovered how to trade a paperclip for a house. So what if it was a bungalow in Saskatchewan? The structure was a real, honest-to-goodness, habitable dwelling, perfect for summer occupancy.

Trading a red paperclip (online) for a pen shaped like a fish, this guy began a journey that, thirteen trades later, led to his final deal for a single-family residence. For purpose of this discussion, I'm going to ignore that he had to stay in Canada, which is a lovely place for anyone who doesn't like to sunbathe and eat enchiladas.

My point is this: Here's someone who must have learned early in life that bartering is better than begging.

If we start early and teach our children how to exchange trivial items for those of greater value, then not only will they someday make good politicians but they'll also become less likely to ever ask to move back home with us.

The best action we can take during Halloween might be to trick rather than treat masked middle-school students. Give them something they'd prefer to trade instead of hoard like pirated treasure. Which brings me to my next major annoyance: Teens who don't realize when they've outgrown the trick-or-treat experience.

I shouldn't have to say this, but children are beyond suitable ages for going door-to-door if, while trick-or-treating, they feel the desire to bring along a date.

Here's a handy test to know when the little darlings are too old to go door-door on Fright Night:

Does the child possess a driver's license?

Is he or she capable of growing underarm hair?

Is he or she wearing a size XXL costume?

Does he or she play varsity sports?

If your child or grandchild can answer "no" to these questions, then by all means, send them my way. I'll be distributing something that's healthy and encourages enterprise. That's right: Paperclips!

Making the Most of the Winter Holidays

Every year, between Thanksgiving and the winter holidays, cooks search for the perfect turkey recipe, one that can be made without consulting Martha Stewart, Betty Crocker, or the Centers for Disease Control and Prevention. To help, I thought I'd share with you my time-tested tidbits for basting a bird.

You'll want your finished product to be visually appealing, not too dry yet fully cooked—or at least thawed. Nothing ruins a festive mood faster than having a guest find a half-frozen neck inside the main entrée.

It's best to cook poultry in a baste that provides a lovely caramel colored glaze, a flavorful hint of sweetness, and just the right proof level to keep the kids quiet. That's why I'm sharing with you my heirloom recipe, Bourbon Turkey Bliss. (I gave you my best pumpkin pie instructions in my book, *Deedee Divine's Totally Skewed Guide to Life*.)

If you should have any trouble following this recipe, please let your physician know. You might be suffering from ADHD (Adult Drinking Holiday Disorder), in which case you'll need to have someone else host the dinner and do all the work.

Here's the recipe:

Bourbon Turkey Bliss

Ingredients:

10-12 lb. turkey, fresh or fully thawed to look that
        way

1 bottle (750 ml), divided, Wild Turkey bourbon

1/3 C honey

1/3 C ketchup

2 Tbsp. dark brown sugar

1 Tbsp. soy sauce

Instructions:

Mix 2 cups of Wild Turkey with honey, ketchup, brown sugar, and soy sauce to form basting sauce. Set aside remaining bourbon.

Brush basting sauce on turkey.

Bake turkey in an oven roasting bag (Do not substitute a dry cleaner bag!) at 325 degrees for approximately ½ hour per pound. That's the turkey's weight, not yours.

Drink remaining bourbon while the turkey cooks.

Have someone else transfer the turkey from oven to serving platter.

Blissfully serves up to 12!

After you've cooked this turkey, you won't even mind singing dumb holiday songs. Is there any tune more monotonous than *The Twelve Days of Christmas*? Why couldn't it have been the "*Five Days of Christmas?*" At least then we could have stopped after a few verses.

I'm no holiday scrooge. But I can't say the same for my husband. He starts getting cranky right after Halloween and doesn't come out of that mood until Valentine's Day. His timing is so obvious that it requires little explanation. On Valentine's Day, he knows he's going to get chocolate.

Knowing the festive fouler he was about to become, one year, I revised the words to *The Twelve Days of Christmas* to better reflect his attitude. Then I sang it to him—which anyone who's ever heard me perform karaoke will agree was sufficient punishment. Here are the words, in case you have a scrooge to whom you'd like to croon this song:

The Twelve Days of a Scrooge's Christmas
(sung to the traditional melody)

On the first day of Christmas, my true love said to me, "I hate this artificial tree."

On the second day of Christmas, my true love said to me, "Two more guests are coming. And I hate this artificial tree."

On the third day of Christmas, my true love said to me, "Three kings are too many. Two more guests are coming. And I hate this artificial tree."

On the fourth day of Christmas, my true love said to me, "Four figure light bills! Three kings are too many. Two more guests are coming. And I hate this artificial tree."

On the fifth day of Christmas, my true love said to me, "Five kids will screa-ea-ea-ea-m. (rest 4 beats) Four figure light bills! Three kings are too many. Two more guests are coming. And I hate this artificial tree."

On the sixth day of Christmas, my true love said to me, "Six hundred was your budget. Five kids will screa-ea-ea-ea-m. (rest 4 beats) Four figure light bills! Three kings are too many. Two more guests are coming. And I hate this artificial tree."

On the seventh day of Christmas, my true love said to me, "Seven months' savings vanished. Six hundred was your budget. Five kids will screa-ea-ea-ea-m. (rest 4 beats) Four figure light bills!

Three kings are too many. Two more guests are coming. And I hate this artificial tree."

On the eighth day of Christmas, my true love said to me, "Eight pies? That's excessive. Seven months' savings vanished. Six hundred was your budget. Five kids will screa-ea-ea-ea-m. (rest 4 beats) Four figure light bills! Three kings are too many. Two more guests are coming. And I hate this artificial tree."

On the ninth day of Christmas, my true love said to me, "Nine more gifts to go?" Eight pies? That's excessive. Seven months' savings vanished. Six hundred was your budget. Five kids will screa-ea-ea-ea-m. (rest 4 beats) Four figure light bills! Three kings are too many. Two more guests are coming. And I hate this artificial tree."

On the tenth day of Christmas, my true love said to me, "Ten sedatives won't help me. Nine more gifts to go? Eight pies? That's excessive. Seven months' savings vanished. Six hundred was your budget. Five kids will screa-ea-ea-ea-m. (rest 4 beats) Four figure light bills! Three kings are too many. Two more guests are coming. And I hate this artificial tree."

On the eleventh day of Christmas, my true love said to me, "Eleven days I've suffered. Ten sedatives won't help me. Nine more gifts to go? Eight pies? That's excessive. Seven months' savings vanished. Six hundred was your budget. Five kids will screa-ea-ea-ea-m. (rest 4 beats) Four figure light bills! Three kings are too many. Two more guests are coming. And I hate this artificial tree."

On the twelfth day of Christmas, my true love said to me, "Twelve cookies and milk aren't free. Eleven days I've suffered. Ten sedatives won't help me. Nine more gifts to go? Eight pies? That's excessive. Seven months' savings vanished. Six hundred was your budget. Five kids will screaˉeaˉeaˉeaˉm. (rest 4 beats) Four figure light bills! Three kings are too many. Two more guests are coming. AND I HATE THIS ARTIFICIAL TREE."

See what I mean about wishing there were fewer verses?

Tainted Toys

As if we didn't have enough stress during the holidays, amid other news reporting hysteria ("Could your microwave popcorn be hazardous to your health?" and "What harmful chemicals are lurking in your frozen bottled water?"), now we have to worry about toxic toys.

Thanks to recalls of painted and magnetic playthings that include such products as dieˉcast cars and miniature doll accessories, I won't be shopping early, this year. I'm too paralyzed by the news to make any purchases. Though, I have to admit, my first thought when I read about the toy recalls was, At last, I have a legitimate reason to quit buying Barbie items!

But more than Barbie-related items have been affected. A substantial number of playthings have been found to have lead paint contamination or magnetic health hazards when consumed. So if you've been allowing your children to eat their toys, in the name of good health, please stop now!

I'm fairly sure my daughter and daughter-in-law are diligent when it comes to what my grandchildren are digesting. But just to be safe, I've been thinking I should line up the grandkids and see if any of them will readily stick to my refrigerator door.

Several types of character merchandise and doll products have been added to the growing list of consumer recalls. Though, I should clue you in on my research. If my son's dog offers any indication of the existing health threat level, there's little to be concerned about. The beast has consumed and digested countless Polly Pocket items with no noticeable effect. That is, other than some comically accessorized dog poo.

Aside from my cavalier approach to this subject, I realize that lead paint and magnet risks are real. It's just that I'm not too sure how far to carry my fears. Do I need to start inspecting every acquisition for the words "Made in China"? Good grief. If I threw away every overseas manufactured item I own, there'd be nothing left inside my house but the TV and stereo—and I'm not even sure about them. But at least they're too big to swallow, right?

Hazardous Holiday Leftovers

I woke up this morning, walked into our family room, and beheld a startling sight. And this time, it wasn't my reflection in the decorative mirror.

"Why is there a toilet seat underneath the Christmas tree?" I asked my husband.

"Because I broke it," he said, as if that explained everything.

"And you set it here because—?

"I'm taking it to Lowe's."

Mentally I noted the Christmas tree is close to the door that leads from the house to the garage. He'd set the oval lid there as a somewhat less than subtle reminder to himself, I presumed. I couldn't help feeling amused by the site of our fully decorated tree, otherwise barren of gifts, and the lone toilet lid beneath its branches. This was a greeting card picture if ever I'd seen one. I could visualize the inscription perfectly: "Hope you get all the crap you want this year!"

Days earlier, my 178-pound spouse had passed through this same room and pronounced, "That's IT. I gained so much weight during Thanksgiving that I actually broke the toilet seat!"

I examined the damage and found only a hairline fracture, which I easily dismissed. That is, until I sat on the splintered fixture and felt a sharp pinch in my posterior.

Thank goodness my man was doing his duty to repair what he'd ruined before my backside suffered another surprise squeeze.

Hubby searched the room for his car keys.

"Don't you need something to put that thing into?" I asked. "You can't just carry it around the store like that."

"Why not? I have to have it with me to make sure I get the right kind of replacement," he said. "Besides, I *cleaned* it."

"Uh-huh. But nobody *knows* you cleaned it," I stressed. "Here," I said, handing him a large gift bag. "Use this."

"That's a Christmas bag!" he declared, as if I might have mistaken it for a man purse. "I can't carry a toilet seat around Lowe's in a Christmas bag."

I puzzled at his logic. He could set a used commode lid underneath a lit Christmas tree, but he drew the line at inserting a broken bathroom fixture into a gift bag? "Oh, right. But you can carry it in your *hands*."

"Sure."

I studied his attire, which I'd only then noticed: a royal blue baseball cap, green polar fleece hockey shirt, chocolate-colored farmer's jacket, black sweatpants (the kind with elastic at the ankles), black socks and casual shoes. There he stood, dressed as I've described, holding a toilet seat in one hand and his car keys in the other.

"Oh, no, you cannot go out of this house like that," I insisted. "Have you *looked* at your clothes?"

"I don't care. I just want to get this project *done*," he declared. "I'm not trying to make an impression on anyone."

That last statement was too much for me. I giggled, then chuckled, and then broke down and howled like a coyote. When I could again speak, I said, "Don't worry, you'll make an impression on anyone who sees you."

I watched him back his car out of the driveway and prayed nobody I knew would be crazy enough to be inside a home improvement store at 8:00 a.m. on a Saturday morning when it was 27 degrees outdoors. And if anyone was, I hoped he or she wasn't equipped with a camera phone.

Who knew that a simple holiday meal could lead to enough leftovers to ruin a man's entire image?

Final Thoughts

Though I've poked a great deal of fun at midlife (which is really the three-quarter mark, but, hey, 60 percent is the new halfway point), there's no better time to reflect upon what we've become and what we're yet to be. That, of course, is dead. It's worth celebrating that we haven't reached the end, I mean. And when I *am* there in that final state of peace and understanding, I hope others (besides my ex-husband) will be joyful too!

I am grateful for every humorous moment God has granted me. And I'm thankful to have survived long enough to share a few of them with you. Especially, I'm blessed to have family who provide me with endless stories to write and, most importantly, rarely read what I've written.

This is where I say thank you, dear reader, for shelling out real dollars for fake advice and crazy commentary. Without your support, I'd be forced to get a paid job and possibly color my own hair.

Finally, I offer my heartfelt appreciation to my loving husband Jim for inspiring me to laugh, encouraging me to persist, and for witnessing but blindly ignoring my ever-changing figure.

Bonus Story

Sometimes I write an essay that just doesn't fit neatly into whatever book I'm currently working on. This is going to be one of those tales, but I wanted to share it with you. Consider this "bonus material," kind of like those extra features offered on DVD movies.

The fact that this essay didn't fit in with the rest of my book's content somehow seemed ideal. After you've read the story, I think you'll see why.

The Final Fit

For many years my father-in-law lived in Cleveland, and my husband and I resided in Texas (which likely contributed to positive family relations). I didn't have the chance to know Big Jim well until his failing health brought him closer to the equator—and my Toyota.

I'd heard stories from my spouse, but it wasn't until I had to chauffer Big Jim to his doctor's office that I learned of his zero tolerance for restricted rides.

To me, a Camry is a comfy car. But for Big Jim, a man whose 6' 4" frame was mostly torso, my vehicle was just another cramped sedan.

"You couldn't afford a car with more head room?" he said when he climbed inside.

I bit my lip to keep from saying, "If you think this is bad, you should see what the taxis are like." But instead I just smiled. He didn't feel well, and the next few months would be my only opportunity to get to know him. I'd heard he had a dry wit and to expect bizarre remarks.

Attempting to be cordial, I asked, "Did you have a good evening, last night?"

His eyes brightened. A sardonic grin crossed his face. "Oh, I sure did," he exclaimed. "I watched a porn movie, and I've never felt better in my life!"

My father-in-law was neither easy to talk to nor understand. Honestly, I couldn't tell if he disliked me or simply loathed my car. It's possible that he merely enjoyed provoking emotions from others because he had trouble displaying many of his own.

Over time, I grew to love Big Jim despite his eccentric behaviors. But I wasn't about to buy another automobile. So he'd need to perfect that head tilt, if I was going to continue providing him lifts.

Big Jim's hankering for more head room became an ongoing war of wills. Soon he began insisting that I drive his Cadillac to the clinic. This motor vehicle had been garaged for months, so I wasn't sure about the engine. And when I drove the beast, I had trouble allowing sufficient room for turns. I kept forgetting to steer as if piloting a small aircraft.

Fitting Big Jim, without complaint, into small spaces became my pastime.

Getting me to conform to his desires became his mission . . . until he departed to that great bulkhead space in the sky.

"When I die, just tie me to a tree out back and let the flies eat me," Big Jim had often teased. But there are laws against obeying these type last wishes. And of course, we knew he hadn't been serious. He'd already prearranged for his body to be cremated. In a moment of stress alleviated by a bout of morbid humor, I caught myself wondering if the burn chamber would be large enough to suit him.

Nevertheless, my mood changed quickly when my husband asked, "Can you go pick up Dad?"

"Pick him up?" I frowned. I'd expected never again to perform that task. "What do you mean?"

"His ashes. They're back. And someone has to retrieve them."

Now, it's not like I hadn't known those ashes would be coming to a temporary rest in my living room. But this was the first time I'd offered more than a fleeting shiver to that idea.

See, nobody on my side of the family has ever been cremated. Though none of my kin would succumb to a midlife facelift, we fully support the postmortem kind. All my deceased relatives have been embalmed to give their loved ones a final chance to say, "Oh, doesn't she look goo-oo-oo-ood?"

"You want me to *touch* his ashes?" I yelped.

"They're in an *urn*," said hubby. "You just have to put it in your car and bring it home."

"I can't do that. Please don't ask me to *touch* those ashes. You know how much I'm already freaked out."

"I have to go to work. The place closes at five o'clock. I can't do it. You're going to have to pick him up. Now quit being a baby and just go *do* it."

Before I could argue further, the door shut between us.

Omigod, Omigod, OMIGOD! I CAN'T DO THIS! It's creepy and disgusting and . . . and . . . so horrifying. I'll be HOLDING DEATH!

Clearly, I was not the best choice for this chore. Unfortunately, there was no one else around to assume the duty. I knew that by the time my husband returned, there'd better be an urn in my car. Or a straightjacket on my arms, which right then seemed entirely achievable.

In the garage I found a square cardboard carton just large enough to hold what I needed to accept, besides my unfortunate availability. My plan was simply to enter the "package pick-up area" and have the attendant place the urn inside my box. This would at least put another layer between my fingertips and Big Jim's charred remains.

At the crematorium, my heart raced while I guppy breathed. A man with a toupee that looked like it could have been stolen from one of the deceased greeted me inside the "showroom."

The attendant directed me to a display rack filled with vases, crates, and urns. "Is this the correct one?" he asked, pointing to a large pewter jar.

"I really don't know," I replied. "I was just asked to retrieve . . . you know . . ." I stared helplessly at the ill-coifed man. "I mean, haven't you already put him in one of these? Visions of this guy maniacally holding a funnel flashed through my mind.

"Oh, no, there's no need to wait," said the representative, "unless you want to consider switching urns."

"No. Whatever was already chosen will be fine," I squeaked.

This man gave me the heebie-jeebies as he led me back to the counter. Then he left momentarily before returning with the urn. Gingerly, he placed Big Jim's contents into the box I'd previously set there. From somewhere beneath the counter, he retrieved something more: a white gift box, just large enough to hold a bangle bracelet. "And I'm afraid," said the agent who now strangely resembled Christopher Walken, "that since your father-in-law was a rather large man . . . um . . . he didn't completely *fit.*"

To make matters worse, which seemed almost impossible right then, the ghoulish guy handed me the tiny carton as though it contained a loose diamond. He explained, "These are the leftover *cremains.*"

After the pipe organ music I subconsciously heard stopped playing, the associate said, "I'm afraid the cremains are still in a somewhat *solid* form, as you're husband stated these were to be buried rather than scattered."

I'm fairly sure what this man saw next was the entrance door closing behind me as I made a dash back to daylight on Planet Normal. Outside, a sunny September afternoon calmed my runaway imagination. I slowed as I neared my vehicle, opened the back door, and slid the urn and *leftovers* inside.

Smiling, I couldn't help but think how perfectly everything fit.

About the Author

Diana Estill's essays have been published in a variety of newspapers, magazines, journals, and books. She is the author of *Driving on the Wrong Side of the Road: Humorous Views on Love, Lust, & Lawn Care,* and *Deedee Divine's Totally Skewed Guide to Life,* a *Foreword* Book of the Year Finalist and International Book Awards Winner. She lives in North Texas with her devoted husband and dominant housecat.